A LIFE
of
MEANING

Also by James Hollis

The Broken Mirror: Refracted Visions of Ourselves

Living Between Worlds: Finding Personal Resilience in Changing Times

Living an Examined Life: Wisdom for the Second Half of the Journey

Hauntings: Dispelling the Ghosts that Run Our Lives

What Matters Most: Living a More Considered Life

Why Good People Do Bad Things: Exploring Our Darker Selves

Finding Meaning in the Second Half of Life

Mythologems: Incarnations of the Invisible World

On This Journey We Call Our Life

Creating a Life: Finding Your Individual Path

The Archetypal Imagination

The Eden Project: In Search of the Magical Other

Swamplands of the Soul: New Life from Dismal Places

Tracking the Gods: The Place of Myth in Modern Life

Under Saturn's Shadow: The Wounding and Healing of Men

The Middle Passage: From Misery to Meaning at Midlife

Harold Pinter: The Poetics of Silence

A LIFE

of

MEANING

RELOCATING
YOUR CENTER OF
SPIRITUAL GRAVITY

JAMES HOLLIS, PhD

sounds true
BOULDER, COLORADO

Sounds True
Boulder, CO 80306

Published 2023

Cover design by Jennifer Miles
Book design by Linsey Dodaro

Printed in Canada

BK06641

Library of Congress Cataloging-in-Publication Data

Names: Hollis, James, 1940- author.
Title: A life of meaning : relocating your center of spiritual gravity /
    James Hollis, PhD.
Description: Boulder, CO : Sounds True, 2023. | Includes bibliographical
    references and index.
Identifiers: LCCN 2022044403 (print) | LCCN 2022044404 (ebook) | ISBN
    9781649630728 (paperback) | ISBN 9781649630735 (ebook)
Subjects: LCSH: Self-actualization (Psychology) | Jungian psychology. |
    Spirituality.
Classification: LCC BF637.S4 H5944 2023 (print) | LCC
    BF637.S4 (ebook) | DDC 158.1—dc23/eng/20220926
LC record available at https://lccn.loc.gov/2022044403
LC ebook record available at https://lccn.loc.gov/2022044404

10 9 8 7 6 5 4 3 2 1

This book is dedicated to the love of my life, Jill, whose constancy and presence have sustained my spirit.

And to our children: Taryn and Tim, Jonah and Seah.

I also wish to thank Liz Harrison and Jennifer Yvette Brown, who saw in these various topics a whole book. And Gretel Hakanson, whose editing and research brought *A Life of Meaning* home.

The time will come
when, with elation
you will greet yourself arriving
at your own door, in your own mirror.

—Derek Walcott, "Love After Love"

Contents

Introduction   ix

   Chapter 1   Discerning the Formative Influences of the Early Days   1

   Chapter 2   When Things Fall Apart in the Midlife Transit   19

   Chapter 3   Shadow Encounters in Personal and Public Life   41

   Chapter 4   The Seven Deadly Sins Through a Psychological Lens   61

   Chapter 5   Dispelling the Ghosts Who Run Our Lives   77

   Chapter 6   Finding Personal Resilience in Times of Change   97

   Chapter 7   Reviewing the Journey   115

   Chapter 8   Living More Fully in the Presence of Mortality   131

   Conclusion   What Does the Psyche Want?   145

Notes   149

Bibliography   153

Index   155

About the Author   161

Introduction

In this book we're going to be exploring doorways to meaning. The topics are loosely arranged in the same sequence as our lives unfold. The topics and insights that you'll be reading about are based on my last forty-plus years as a practicing Jungian analyst. In my early professional life, I was an academic and professor of humanities. At midlife, I retrained in Switzerland at the Jung Institute in Zurich and became a practicing Jungian analyst. Along the way, it's been my privilege to meet and work with many folks in psychotherapy and of course to observe, read, and think about these matters. The book is based on asking questions that really matter in our lives because I believe large questions get us a larger life, a life that takes us to places that engage the mind, spirit, and soul. This anthology includes some of the most requested popular topics through the years and the issues that seem to come up repeatedly in the context of individual psychotherapy.

The tone of this book is a bit more informal than most of my books as this collection of essays was first recorded at the Sounds True studios in Boulder, Colorado, in 2019. Through the years, many listeners requested a complementary text to review, and so I was happy when the editors of Sounds True decided that was a good idea also. In a few cases, the text has been changed for purposes of clarity, but all in all, this printed version is a faithful rendering of the original oral versions.

James Hollis
Washington, DC
2022

1

Discerning the Formative
Influences of the Early Days

I n this chapter, we're going to be considering this journey we call our life and
discerning some of the formative influences of our early days, particularly
those that linger with us and continue to influence our decisions, perhaps
forcing us into some decisions and choices and keeping us from others. Carl Jung
believed that this life is a short pause between two mysteries. That's a pretty good
definition of life, and to which I might add that our summons is to make this short
pause as luminous as we can. And how do we do that?

ASKING QUESTIONS THAT MATTER

The path of personal growth and development is not found so much in finding the
answers, which we all certainly wished for as youths, because the answers we do
find at best serve only for a little while or are someone else's answers. Life is forever evolving, and yesterday's truth is tomorrow's prison. You may recall the old
folk wisdom that no prisons are more confining than "those we know not we're
in." Rather, I believe we get a larger life by asking larger questions and keeping
those questions before us—not from settling for the available answers, which
ultimately prove limiting.

Answers tell us where we've been. Questions get us on our journey, and I've
often said to people in psychoanalysis, "This is not about curing you because
you're not a disease, you're a process. This is about making your life more interesting to you—a life full of adventure, a life full of daily choices that create and
express your values."

When we were toddlers, given our dependency, our questions were understandably survival based: Who's going to take care of me? What do I need to do

to keep your approval? How do I stay out of trouble with you? Can you teach me what the world is about? While those questions might remain germane to our well-being, if they're still governing our lives today, then we are unwittingly in service to infantilizing agendas and perpetuating that initial dependency instead of gaining a measure of sovereignty in our lives.

So in this book we will be asking different questions—questions designed to help us find those pockets of dependency that persist and perhaps better deal with our resistances and stuck places. This exploration of questions will certainly be followed by some ideas about finding your answers, and I hope they will help you do so. But if you use my answers, they may not apply to your own life. So be sure to find your own answers.

So much of what we do today is driven by, or at least influenced by, our internalized stories—those fragmentary personal narratives and "splinter scripts" that define who we are, who "others" are, and how we are expected to relate to one another. Some of those stories are quite overt and conscious as we were specifically taught to think, feel, and behave by our elders, our teachers, and our societies. Other narratives were quietly assembled by us day in and day out until invisibly they became who we are, or at least who we think we are.

If we're going to understand ourselves, make choices from a deeper place, and make authentic choices rather than serve predetermined behaviors, we have to become conscious of how those stories operate in our daily lives. Now, as you know, the problem with the unconscious is that it is unconscious. In fact, we can't even say for certain it exists, and yet aspects of our choices, our hidden lives, keep spilling into the world. We leave a trail of choices and their consequences behind every day. Who or what agencies within are making those choices?

Something is running the show, monitoring our breathing process, our digestive process, our emotional process. Something brings dreams to us every night. Something is going on in there. So we have to try to address what's happening in the unconscious. How can we work with it in a more deliberate and thoughtful way? Of course, we can only make something conscious when it has entered the world as a behavior pattern, a dream image, a somatic complaint, or a projection.

DREAMS AND THE REALM OF THE UNCONSCIOUS

A common question I hear from new clients is, "So where do I start in this analysis of my journey?" I always say, "Well, start with your patterns."

You don't wake up in the morning and while brushing your teeth and looking in the mirror, say, "Today I'm going to do the same stupid things I've done for decades." But chances are you will. By the end of the day, you will have replicated some of those choices and some of those values, and the consequences pile up.

Eventually, we begin to realize that what we do is "logical" based on the premise from which it comes. We don't do crazy things; we do logical things. Many of our premises, many of our early stories, are fictions. There may have been a time when they were useful, constructive, or protective fictions. But even so, they bind us to a disabling, disempowered past. When we look at our patterns, we have an invitation to work backward into the realm of the unconscious, that realm wherein so many of our choices are actually made.

Sometimes it's important to listen to what others tell us about our behaviors and our patterns, if we can bear listening, bear taking seriously the critique of others. It takes a certain amount of strength to be able to hear someone else's critique of us. Then as that old Eastern proverb stated it, "Bless those who curse and revile you, for they shall prove your greatest teachers." Well, talk is cheap. That's difficult at times, but we do learn from those who offer critiques of our behaviors.

Along with our patterns we also have dreams that offer us correctives, challenges, contradictions. Sleep research tells us that in an ordinary sleep cycle, we average about six dreams per night. You might say, "Well, I don't remember that many dreams," "I don't dream," or "I never remember my dreams." And that may be true for you. But it's also true that nature does not waste energy. It has a purpose in this dream formation, and I think that purpose is to help us work through the magnitude of stimuli that bombard us on a daily basis, to help us assimilate and metabolize our experiences, even if we don't work with what the meaning might be.

But if we do begin to pay attention to our dreams, we realize there is a profound myth-making work afoot there, a mythopoeic process that is not only forming impressions but actually commenting on our lives. Most radically, there's some kind of informing intelligence that is looking at our lives, offering its perspective, and wishing to communicate with us. Would it not make sense from time to time to stop and pay attention and listen to what dreams are trying to tell us?

In addition to our patterns and dreams, we have to learn to respect and to read our symptoms. Symptoms are autonomous intrusions into the flow of daily life, and they're important clues—clues that point to the astonishing fact that our psyche is observing, evaluating, and critiquing how our harried executives upstairs on the floor called consciousness are managing our lives. Symptoms often are, in a sense, indications that our psyche is not amused by our choices and so it offers alternatives.

Finally, in looking backward into the realm of the unconscious, we have to pay attention to what we project onto others. A projection is an unconscious mechanism. We don't know that we've done it. A projection is where our intrapsychic material—an agenda, a set of expectations, or perhaps a fear-based response—is triggered. Maybe we want that person to do something, then when they cease to do that, or they fail to live up to our expectations, we often feel confusion and dismay, maybe even anger toward the other for not living up to our expectations. In that case, we have to say to ourselves, *All right, what is it I put out on that person that has now come back to me? I'm accountable for that. What do I need to learn? What unfinished business does my eroded projection now ask of me?*

For example, often in intimate relationships we expect the other to fix things for us, take care of us, or make us feel good about ourselves. If we really examine those projections, that myriad agenda of expectations, we begin to realize, if we are honest, mature, and accountable, *Oh, that's my job. I have to do that.* Lifting our unfinished business off of someone else is truly a heroic and loving thing to do.

We need also to remember the distinction between the Self with a capital *S* and our "sense of self." Our sense of self is essentially the accumulation of all the stories that evolved as we tried to make sense of our lives. So, for example, if a person experienced emotional invasion from others, challenging socioeconomic circumstances, or other factors over which they had no control, they concluded that they are essentially powerlessness in the face of the large challenges of life. Given that internalized narrative, they reflexively project such power discrepancies onto others and thereby serve the old narrative, which, again, produces patterns. While we live these patterns every day, when we step outside them and take a look, we often rationalize, *That is just who I am* or *That is how life is.* Little do we realize, until perhaps the consequences pile high, that we are still captive to early formative experiences and are not exercising the powers of the emergent adulthood we in fact possess.

From the ego's limited purview, the Self is a kind of natural, organic autonomous other. It's the totality of our nature seeking to express itself. But our sense of self is conditional, acculturated, and very, very provisional. It's influenced by our time and place, religious and educational backgrounds, family-of-origin dynamics, and so often is limited by the child's perspective rather than the adult's far more capacious possibilities of choice.

While our sense of self makes many of our choices for us, the Self is always seeking its expression through us. When it is violated, as it so often is, it pathologizes and creates symptoms. But more about that later.

Our sense of self is slowly built from our earliest life and our earliest encounters, repeated and reinforced, corrected and altered and ratified by our environmental pressures. Over time, it takes on the status of an operational personality—semiautonomous, reflexively triggered, and driven by the adaptive strategies of the past. But is it our life? The one intended for us by the gods?

RELATIONAL PATTERNS OF OUR EARLIEST STORIES

Let's ask some of the questions that begin to probe our sense of self and lift some of the layers to glimpse the mechanisms that lie within each of us. Perhaps the most obvious questions are: How do we come to know ourselves, and how do we come to know others?

From the first moment of our lives, profound questions are urgent: Who are you? Who am I? Are you safe, reliable, absent, punitive, invasive, abandoning? What sense can I make of what I'm experiencing? Because our well-being is tied to understanding, we began to "story" our world. (Yes, you read that right; I just converted a noun into a verb.) We make a story out of an active process in service to constructing a predictable world for ourselves.

Our stories are our provisional interpretations of what is going on and what it might mean to us. These provisional narratives are fueled with emotion within us and embodied in a somatic registry that never forgets. Thus, we all grow attached to a partial script—a script that may keep showing up in our later lives or might slip into oblivion to be replaced by other, more powerful scripts. No matter how competent we are in the outer world, how "successful" we are in the eyes of the world, most of us, most of the time, are on automatic pilot. In other words, we're in service to reflexive strategies that are designed to meet our needs, manage anxiety, and stay out of harm's way as best we can.

Our systemic relational patterns arise from our earliest stories—stories with which we have lived so long that we consider them reality rather than provisional fictions, stories in which we are locked until we recognize them. For example, we all know of people who change partners, jobs, or locations and then unwittingly repeat their patterns of choice. Then they are surprised to encounter the same dreary outcomes. Seldom do we recognize that we ourselves are the common factor in our catalog of relational and professional choices. What we encounter daily is radically new and yet is seen through the lens of history—a lens whose refraction was ground by the earliest stories of trust, betrayal, expectation, disappointment, controller-compliant behaviors, and so on. Perhaps you've lived a similar scenario yourself. We all have, somewhere on this journey.

In such cases, our formative stories reframe our present moment in service to the old expectations, even scanning for certain kinds of people with whom to reenact, and the new possibilities are subordinated to familiar repetitive strategies. Then we find, to our surprise and dismay, that we are back in the same place as before.

For a long time, psychologists have noted that our repetitive tendency is enacted through powerfully functional mechanisms, which we carry with us as tools to make possible sense of the utterly unique, utterly foreign world that confronts us in every new moment of choice. They're called *projection* and *transference*.

Projection happens when the psyche has been triggered by something. For example, whenever I meet a person, a whole field of history is activated. Different aspects of my history will be triggered based on the context, the appearance of that person, and the general expectations of the situation. And, whether I know it or not, up comes a story from the past. That story is unconsciously projected onto that person. Unknowingly I flood that person with my own psychological material. Because this transaction is unconscious, I have no way of knowing how I have distorted the other and constructed a provisional script. While that framing of reality, that story, may have helped me make sense of the world, today it prejudices the new reality and brings about the same old, same old. Even if I wish to understand why I might cling to my old story, its reappearance prejudices the new situation and imposes upon it the data and worldviews of the old.

Shortly after the projection has occurred, it is followed by transference. Transference happens when I respond to that person in an old familiar way: How did I act in the past that may have seemed productive or protective or helpful in some way? Transference points to our tendencies to employ the old stratagems of the old stories because they are what we bring to the table. Projection and transference, on one hand, help us build on our experience and provide continuity to our days. On the other hand, they condition and prejudice our reactions in our relational patterns with people. In short, they are the architects of our patterns, the repetitive responses that may or may not have once served but today bind us to our less capacious past.

So when we ask: What stories do we carry into our relationships? What stories do we serve over and over? It's very hard to get at those answers because the stories are often operating out of very early moments in our development, long before we had the capacity to step outside ourselves and see our choices objectively. In fact, we're more than one story or one strategy for adaptation and survival; we are many. In changing circumstances and provocations, we will employ various forms of coping skills, whether consciously or not. The most pervasive, often the most damaging, are those we know not we're serving, for then their autonomy is reinforced.

THE EXISTENTIAL THREATS OF OVERWHELMENT AND ABANDONMENT

Our stories are the result of two core existential threats to our survival and well-being: overwhelment and abandonment. Over time, these patterns, acquired in our formative years, often get locked in as reflexive responses. Each pattern then has the potential of becoming a "way of life." You will probably be able to find all of them at work in your life. They will vary according to our age, maturation, and situation, but all of them have been utilized as means of adapting to the world, protecting ourselves, and getting our needs met as best we can with the limited powers at our disposal.

The smaller we are, the more often we experience encounters with situations and people as overwhelming. All of us at some time felt pretty powerless in a powerful, autonomous world around us.

Out of that encounter with the magnitude of the "other," there are basically three patterns of coping, adapting, and making do the best we can in response to that overwhelment. These responses are very logical responses to the large powerful "other" (the world). First is avoidance. Second is the search for power to contend with the powerful "other." The third is giving the other what it wants or seems to demand.

There are several subcategories of avoidance. First there is simple avoidance, where we just don't deal with things and routinely avoid difficult and conflictual encounters. Second is procrastination, where we deliberately postpone or delay the troubling encounter. Third, we employ suppression, where we put things aside consciously and deliberately, and imagine that we will deal with them in the future, but we may not. Then, as Freud pointed out, there is repression, where to protect the fragility of ego consciousness, the psyche reflexively pushes things into the unconscious. Then we sometimes get caught in projections onto others in which we might relate to them in disempowered ways. Further, we have various forms of numbing—from drugs and alcohol to exhaustion. We live in a world that offers us distraction from what troubles us. We can even disassociate, where we find alternative modes of reality to live in as a form of protecting us from the imminent pressures of the present moment. These protective mechanisms are patterns of avoidance, all logical responses to the experience of, or expectation of, the large powerful other.

Second in our response to overwhelment, we may slip into the power complex. Power itself is neutral. Power is the energy to address life's tasks. But when caught in an old story—a complex—the story can often have a life of its own, an autonomy that produces all kinds of problematic patterns. The power complex sometimes expresses itself by seeking overt power over the other. You see it in brute force, controlling behaviors, manipulation, and passive-aggressive behaviors in a relationship. The benign form of that power need expresses itself through learning and growth, and greater management of one's life. That's why we read books such as this one—in an effort to get greater understanding of our life, to have potentially more power over its management.

The third adaptive pattern to the threat of overwhelment by the "other" is essentially to give the world what it wants—to get along, you go along. Most of us were conditioned and taught to be good children, which meant to be adaptive and cooperative. Of course, society depends upon a certain measure of give-and-take; we all know that. But it gets pretty sticky if we realize that we are continuously compromising our values in order to fit in, to be safe, to stay out of harm's way. *Codependent* is what we call people who reflexively transfer power to others and find themselves in compliant patterns, even as they lament their familiar position of subordination. Sooner or later, they experience great chagrin at their repetitive choice to once again ratify their sense of powerlessness, but they remain locked in a story that once seemed protective but later becomes constrictive.

The other existential threat is abandonment: there's never enough to fill our archaic needs. Our needs and desires are infinite, and the capacity of our parents and the world is finite. There's always a gap there. But if there's been a large enough gap, we will often have some kind of childhood identification with those deficits, leading to a substantial wound to our self-esteem. In other words, every child tends to think, *I am what happened to me* or *I am my atmosphere* or *I am what my world seems to be saying to me.*

Children are deeply shaped by the dynamics of their family. They're defined by poverty, racism, sexism, and so forth—all of which are outside them, of course. But the child experiences them as *These are somehow about me and are an expression of me.* These wounds to self-esteem—and we all have them—show up most commonly in forms of self-sabotage or the avoidance of real choices in life; taking life on and fighting for what we want; self-denying, self-defeating behaviors; or overcompensation via grandiosity—"Look how wealthy I am. Look at how achieved my children are." All are compensatory for inner feeling of inadequacy.

The second adaptive pattern to the abandonment threat is the power complex, but this time in a quite different form from the overwhelment pattern.

The power complex shows up here when, operating out of our narcissistic wounds, we seek control over others. It's most insidiously found in a parent's manipulation of children. Parents will often want their children to grow up and be very much like them, endorsing their religious values, their cultural preferences, and so forth, not realizing how invasive and destructive this is. We all have narcissistic wounds, but the question is, to what degree do we impose them upon other people in the expectation of their taking care of it for us?

The third threat response pattern is an inordinate need for self-assurance, an excessive neediness. We all have needs. That's normal, that's human, but urgent neediness as we know tends to drive people away.

So when we look at those six patterns in response to witnessing the magnitude of the world into which we have been thrust, of overwhelment and abandonment (avoidance, search for power, compromising our values, diminished self-worth, the power complex, excessive neediness), we have to also start seeing how many of our patterns of avoidance keep piling up.

Avoidance always has consequences. To find out what those consequences are, ask: Where do my power issues show up in dealing with others? Or where do I become overly compliant?

I've often said I should start a new 12-step program called Recovering Nice Persons Anonymous. We would get together periodically and talk about how reflexively we compromise our values in order to be acceptable, to fit in.

In the face of abandonment, we frequently internalize deficiencies as wounds to self-esteem. How do they show up? Do they lead to self-defeating patterns? Or do we find ourselves having to somehow pump up and promote our sense of importance? I think about that every time I fly. There are these lines and classes of elite passengers who get to get on first. I think, *Well, we're all in the same plane, we're all arriving at the same time, we hope.* What does all this airline ritual serve except treating that sense of psychological deficit? Or the power complex, where we use others for narcissistic needs; or our needs are such that they are demanding and controlling, and ultimately, of course, push people away, achieving exactly the opposite of what we wanted. The needier the person, the likelier the pressure on those around them to meet those needs. Over time, this extra burden tends to push people away, leaving the individual with even less affirmation and support.

INVISIBLE POWERS AND PRESENCES

Of course, just as there are wounding trauma-based strategies, we may have experienced supportive parents or relatives or a teacher or coach. So we also have to ask: What supported me during childhood? What gave me a sense of inherent value or legitimacy, or where I didn't feel I had to earn love, approval, validation? What informed me or confirmed my right to be here, to feel what I feel and desire what I desire? What gave me permission to go seek for what I want in this life? Do I remember to draw upon those assets when I meet difficulties in life, as inevitably we do? If I don't feel legitimate as a person, inherently worthy, why not? Is that the old archaic story at work again? If not that, what later assumption did I make whereby I construed life's setbacks and disappointments as being a demeaning message about me?

I often find people don't feel legitimate or inherently worthy. They frequently feel provisionally tentative and at the mercy of their environment. Gaining a sense of worth and recovering personal authority thus becomes the single most important task of the second half of life. From our personal authority, or lack thereof, our choices rise, our consequences multiply, and our lives course onward in their uncertain ways. Too often we identify who we are by what happened to us.

As I mentioned, children are often defined or limited directly by poverty, racism, sexism, and a thousand other events or contexts that have nothing to do with a child's soul or its potential for the expression of life force. Often the desired outcome of therapy is the discovery that we are not what happened to us but what we chose to become. This transformation of consciousness makes a huge difference in our sense of permission to live the life we wish and to take the risks necessary to fulfill our potential. Another way of putting it is, "I am what is wanting expression through me, not what happened to me."

As a Jungian analyst, I've often tried to put a wedge between what happened to a person and who they think they are—their old reductive and restrictive stories. It seems impossible at times to believe, but it is true that what happened to us was what happened "out there." What happened "out there" is not who we are. What happened was seldom about us. It was about someone else's problems, someone else's limitations. Your life is and always has been a separate journey. Separating your journey from your history is difficult but essential to a free and fuller life.

Another question to ask of yourself is this: *Who did I think I was then, at that stage of my maturation? And what did I think I needed to do with my life or that life was going to ask of me?* Often we watch those around us, family members in particular, for clues as to how we are to behave and what is expected of us. Additionally, other cultural influences, ethnicity, religious instruction, the zeitgeist, and so on gave us powerful messages. These collective messages often separate a person from their guiding instincts and become a by-product of one's environment, the carrier of the germ of the unlived life.

For example, when I was a child and throughout my youth, my father worked in a factory building tractors and graders, a job he hated. He also worked on weekends, delivering coal to families. He never once complained in my presence. He accepted his life, and he bore it as courageously as he could. But I could see and feel the repressed emotion. And so I too learned from him to repress, contain, not express what was going on inside. Naturally, that emotion never went away. It just boiled inside and demanded an appointment with me later in life. When it returned at midlife, it took form as a depression, the ache of living a provisional life, an adaptive life, and not honoring what was surging inside in search of expression. When any of us lose contact with these feeling responses, we also lose contact with a powerful source of insight as to how our souls, our psyches, are responding to the circumstances of our lives. The old cliché of being in touch with one's feelings is accurate, for we do not create feelings. They are the autonomous, evaluative responses to how our psyche is experiencing our life, rather than what our noisy complexes insist is correct living.

This self-estrangement, this disconnect, causes us to become strangers to ourselves. Such an inner separation is the fertile ground for depression, self-medication, and a life of conditioned repetitive responses with all their accumulating consequences.

As I'm sure is true for you, when I was child, there were all kinds of messages from the environment. While I was perfectly safe in America's heartland during World War II, I fully believed, based on what I saw around me, that my role in life was to grow up and be a soldier and kill somebody or be killed in return. That led to many troubled nights for that child, even as he was safe.

Yet another question to ask yourself is: *If I could change them now, what choices would I revisit?* As we know, seldom does life allow us a do-over, but what would you do over? What do you know now that you didn't then? This is not to foster regret or recrimination or blaming yourself or others; rather, it's a forensic exploration of the interior architecture of our choices and our feelings in life. However, if we don't recognize some of those false turns and perhaps acknowledge the necessity of them, then we're likely to be their servant for good. We can ask ourselves, *What powers or presences stood, perhaps invisibly, at the junctures of my life and caused the train of life to go down one track rather than the others? Are those presences still operational in my life?* It is so important to construct this archaeological examination of the causal factors in these critical decisions because they're still present in us, still possibly exercising a hand on the lever that sends our life down one track or another.

In the face of large influences, messages, and powerful stories, we really only have three choices in general. The first and most common is to repeat the implicit message. In the face of powerfully reinforced stories, we tend to repeat. That's what causes patterns in our lives, even intergenerational patterns, as things roll down from one person's experience into another's.

The second choice is that we run in the opposite direction when we sense something dangerous or difficult. We overcompensate. Every time a person says, "But I won't be like my mother" or "I'm not going to live my father's life," we're still in some way being defined by that which is external to us—someone else's life.

Third, we try to find a way to fix it. We can fix it through a life of distraction, of busyness—a life of being busy at every moment so we don't reflect on these matters. Or we can try to medicate these inner conflicts in various ways.

But in every case, these messages, these stories, are playing a role in our life. Are we repeating them? Are we compensating for them, or we're trying unconsciously to fix them? Therefore, we have to ask this question: What were the formative messages that show up still in my current life? And here's the pragmatic question: What do they make me do, or what do they keep me from doing?

VOCATION AS A SUMMONS OF THE SOUL

In a related forum, we might ask, Why, when we do the right thing as best we can, doesn't it seem to work out? Or why does it never feel right? Sometimes we even have to acknowledge, even welcome, psychopathology.

We live in a world that wishes to rid us as quickly as possible of suffering through a behavioral change or a pill. But stop and think for a moment about the word *psychopathology*. *Psyche* is the Greek word for soul. *Pathos* refers to suffering. *Logos* means "word" or "expression." So psychopathology is literally the expression of the suffering of the soul. Wouldn't it make sense to stop and pay attention? And remember also the etymology of the word *therapy*. *Therapeuein* means "to listen or attend to psyche, the soul"—to pay attention to rather than suppress psychopathology and to ask, "What is the soul trying to say to me?"

Psychopathology, of course, can get our attention and make us reconsider. Sometimes it even offers us a path through the dark wood to a different journey. That was my experience at midlife when I began asking the question, "What does the psyche want?" This question is the beginning of healing the vast split each of us carries within. Then we realize that the ego is obliged to relinquish its privileged position as the regal potentate to be the servant of an even higher power. That's why this work is not narcissistic. It's about finding something worthier of our service than our inherited stories or those adaptive patterns that bind us to a disabling past.

We achieve many, many things from our conscious functioning in the world. We need our egos to help us mediate our engagement with others, to provide intentionality and moral choice, and to bind our days together with a semblance of continuity and consistency. But as all the ancient prophets, poets, and philosophers warn, when the ego gets inflated, when it thinks it's really the boss, then the system is in trouble.

That reminds me of the old story on how the gods died. Reportedly, Yahweh told them that he was God, and they all died laughing. Well, if we think ordinary consciousness is in control of our lives, then how do we account for all those stuck places? Or the times when we violated our professed values, the times when we hurt others or ourselves? Psychopathology, then, is the autonomous protest of our inner life to the conditions of our outer life, whether from our choices or whether imposed upon us by circumstances or others. So there's always the invitation to consider: What does the soul want? This question is not designed for our ego's comfort, for it often will put us in harm's way. It can lead us away from the consensual reality or community approval and sometimes make our journey very lonely.

Most of the people whom we admire in history did not have easy lives; rather, we admire them for what they embodied through their lives. They won their way through, through the difficulties, to bring those values, those witnesses, into this world and thereby enriched all of us. Vocation, for example, is one of those summonses of the soul. We all do jobs to earn our living, but what is our vocation, our vocatus, our "calling"? Our calling often requires commitment, discipline, courage, consistency, and persistence. It's not about comfort, fitting in, being normal at all.

Recently, I recognized a kindred spirit in the words of the late novelist Dame Hilary Mantel of England. She said that she never counted on inspiration to come and tap her on the shoulder. Rather, she trusted her own work ethic and vigilance to observe and utilize what she was finding in the process of hammering out a text. I admire that because in it I see a commitment not to the ego's comfort but to its sacrifice in service to vocation.

People have said to me, because of having written many books, "Well, writing's got to be easy for you." I think, *Why would you think that?* Writing is what I do at the end of having seen patients all day. Writing is what I do rather than watch the ball game or something else because something inside me insists on it. I've learned I'm better off serving that which wishes to be served. The novelist Thomas Mann concluded that writing is an act that's especially difficult for those who are writers.

Your vocation is really not about a job, per se. It's about what is truly worthy of your commitment, your service. I love Mantel's saying about writing because it makes clear the necessity of commitment to whatever we're called. The calling itself is a mystery that comes from someplace deep within the soul. Inspiration—the word *inspirare* translates as "the breath within"—means to have the breath of the gods moving through us. What we are called to do is often not what we do for a living. So one must always ask the questions: *Is what I am doing in accord with my vocation? Does it serve the calling of my soul? Or is it in service to the ego under one of its many occupations by my stories or the world's stories imposed upon me?* In addition, Mantel's praise of eternal vigilance is a reminder of the obligatory discipline of self-awareness. We are forever discovering new things about ourselves, about others, and about how things come into being through us. Not to be vigilant is to be asleep, on automatic pilot, and dangerous to self and others.

So our job is to pay attention; *therapeuein*—to listen, to attend to. When we are in accord with the terrain of our inner life, we experience supportive energy, a feeling of confirmation, and most of all, most elusive but most necessary, a sense of meaning, fulfillment, and purpose. When we're off track, in service to those old adaptive patterns, we have to force matters and make things happen, and it gets harder and harder and harder. We know that's always the path to depression and burnout down the line.

We were all born knowing what is right for us. It was called *instinct*, but when we were tiny, dependent, vulnerable, at the mercy of the world around us, we had to adapt to the fate into which we were thrown. As Jung often mentioned, most of our troubles come when we have lost contact with our guiding instincts, that energy within each of us that's in service to becoming who we are in the world. The philosopher Friedrich Nietzsche also called us "the sick animal." So we all get into trouble via what once protected us or seemed to protect us and at least seemed necessary.

We launch the recovery of our possible journey by asking these questions I've just suggested. We have to ask them throughout our lives because we don't solve these problems once and for all. They persist and insinuate themselves in new ways, new forms, and new subtleties. The older I get, the more I see the reappearance of these archaic stories in my patients and in myself. We can never assume we have arrived. It is when we have that hubristic confidence that we know who we are and why we're making all the choices we're making that we are most in the grip of the old stories.

Since the 1980s, research has told us that decisions are often made in the brain before we've even begun to consider that we have a decision to make consciously. That's a scary thought. For example, a ball is headed toward your head; it is seen, registered, and responded to in the millisecond before you say to yourself, *Duck!* I don't know about you, but I find that fact both reassuring and disconcerting. It's reassuring in that it tells me we have operational systems that are protecting us, that we know very little about, and that perhaps have allowed us to survive as a species on the planet. On the other hand, it's still another affront to the ego's fantasy that it's in charge.

That is what these questions are designed to do—to lift us out of the debris and distractions of daily life, to bring us to greater consciousness, to help us all sift and sort, and to lift the multilayered psyche in its mechanism into the light of awareness. That's our project here. That's how we begin the process of getting our lives back. It's humbling work, not inflationary. It doesn't make us feel good. Simplistic, feel-good theologies and psychologies let us down sooner or later. But this summons to personal accountability, to courage, and to persistence gives us a steady job. It brings with it the quiet dignity of living our journey and not someone else's. I submit to you that's worth the price of the ticket and the path to making this journey we call our lives even more luminous.

STIRRING THE PROCESS

You may have been asking yourself, *What are some of the specific practices or disciplines I might undertake to facilitate this process?* First I would like you to review the questions that I've raised above. They're basic questions, I admit, but they will begin to sift and sort and lift the material up out of the unconscious. The etymology of the word *analysis*, as in analyzing the "psyche," comes from a Greek verb that means "to stir up from below," like stirring up a riverbed or a bowl of soup to see what veggies float to the surface. So, we stir the process.

Once you really stir the process, you are going to find the things that keep floating to the surface. You might wake at three in the morning and there's a thought there, an idea; write it down. Or you might find that this process triggers dreams. Write those dreams down and pay attention to them. Try to disidentify from the ego perspective when you look at those dreams. You might ask: *Now, why would the psyche have chosen this person or this situation? What are my associations with that?* That's how we get around the ego's effort at its exercising its sovereignty over this material and begin to realize that it's always but one complex floating among many—an important and useful one, yes, but only one of many. Using a journal, paying attention to your dreams, meditating, and particularly looking at the patterns of your life work backward in that forensic examination may well lead to opening alternative pathways for you.

Remember that all the things you do are logical. The emotional premise or story may have made sense at the time it came into being. Perhaps it was a child's fantasy or fear not based on any reality. Yet it gets locked in and reinforced and therefore becomes a sort of operative assumption on our part. Ask yourself: *What is the story from which this comes? How do I see that today as an adult? How do I approach that with the wherewithal, the tools of rationality, comparative experience, sense of alternatives, and most importantly, discovering a reservoir of resilience that the adult has that often the child did not have? How do I revision that story, recontextualize it? And what kind of story leads to a larger life, a more satisfying life?* I think we all know the answers to these questions. Jung said once that there was virtually no one, even of all those who came to see him, who didn't know at some level what they needed to do with their life. I tend to find that true as well. We may not know what we know, but it's lying just beneath the surface.

So we have to find anew what we already know. We need to pay attention to a process that allows us to figure out what we know because it has long known us and waited for our recognition and investment. We have to find the courage to face what we know to be true and to make those changes. Then we go back to those questions and ask: How did I understand this then? How do I understand this today? What are the capacities I have today to make alternative choices? When we do this, we gain a greater purchase on our adulthood. We realize that, as the Swedish poet Gunnar Ekelöf once wrote, these things are like a giant ocean liner, so far offshore that we can't see it. But we can tell it's there because the waves start lifting and lapping against the shore and then recede, and we realize something large has just passed. Sometimes working with the unconscious is that subtle; sometimes it's that difficult. And we have to ask: Why did I make that choice? Where did that come from in me? Where metaphorically have I been here before?

The psyche's like an analog computer. Every moment is new, but it is always saying, *What do I know about this? Where have I been here before?* The data search is instantaneous. There are thousands of metaphoric "little people" running around downstairs, combing the files, and saying, "All right, what does this look like? What does our experience tell us?" And up pops the nearest approximation from our history from our thesaurus of experience, and from that we make choices. And guess what? It's often the same old, same old; the repetitious patterns. From those patterns we realize the incredible power of those formative stories. At the same time, we realize there are other formative stories that are seeking to enter the world through us. Where do those stories come from? That's what Jung meant by the Self.

The Self is the transcendent organic wisdom of nature seeking its expression. Nature is not particularly interested in our comfort, our fitting in, or our being successful in conventional terms. It's more about serving its own end. Nature serves nature. Ironically, the formation of our ego that allows us to create a presence in the external world often resists this summons back to an honest service of what wishes to enter the world through us.

It's out of that humbling experience that we experience our own spiritual depth. We experience meaning. We experience a sense of rightness that can only come to us when we're standing in right relationship to our own soul. We can't manufacture that. We can't create it from a driven programmatic standpoint. We have to ask the question: What is psyche asking of me? Then we try to live what emerges as best we can. When we do so, it makes a huge difference in our lives and becomes part of the legacy we pass on to our children, to our families, and to our fellow citizens.

2

When Things Fall Apart in the Midlife Transit

In this chapter, we're going to consider why sometimes things fall apart when our presumed center cannot hold. Often our stories that we work so hard to serve, and perhaps serve faithfully, no longer serve us. Sometimes the map that we had of the world, which may or may not have worked very well heretofore, proves no longer effective today.

WHEN THE CENTER CANNOT HOLD

When I came back from my Jungian training in Zurich at midlife and started working with individuals in the United States, I saw a wide range of people in ages from approximately thirty to sixty-five and a mixture of women and men. I began to see that while they came with a different set of presenting issues, each one had all kinds of history at play in their lives. Each had a different kind of understanding of themselves and the world, but there was one thing in common to each one of them.

Their worldview, their understanding of themselves and the world, their sense of identity, or perhaps their script was now played out or exhausted. In each case, something was dying and nothing was yet there to replace that eroding worldview. In each case, there was a sense of a terrible in-between, where we find ourselves caught between what we believe to be the case and what often presents itself in a disquieting way, or between who we were and what is wanting to enter the world through us.

One of my clients was a forty-year-old woman who was concerned that she might have a terminal illness. Her outer life had been well served, her last child had gone off into adulthood, and she had a stable life. However, she realized something was missing in her life. She told me of a dream that was very troubling to her. In the dream, she's about to have her first therapy session, but she has her hair done up in old-fashioned curlers. The therapist was coming to see her in the hospital, and she didn't want her therapist to see those curlers on her head. In other words, my client didn't want the therapist to really see what was going on in her head. While she's waiting, a relative comes to her and says very sweetly, "Joanne, it's time to die." And she says to her relative, "Oh, okay." And that's the end of the dream.

In the dream, she accepts this announcement that it's time to die. You can see why, from an ego standpoint, her concern was that she had some kind of terminal illness. I said, "Well, we all have a terminal illness but not likely for a few decades." At forty, and in good health, she had no reason to believe she had a physical illness. She literalized the concept of death rather than saw it symbolically. (The ego often falls into this trap, which is one reason interpreting our own dreams is so difficult.)

When we look closely at that tendency, we can see the natural ambivalence we have toward self-examination. Her dream was refueling her anxieties: *Is there something wrong with me? Am I ill? Do I belong in a hospital? What will someone think if they see my thought process; will they critique me?* But then that's overshadowed by the relative coming to her to announce that it's time for her to die and her very meekly accepting it. What was critical here was her recollection that that relative was probably the single most supportive person in her extended family, the one person who was always on her side.

First, we had to stop and admire the ingenuity of the psyche to send the person from her historic cast of characters who was most supportive of her growth and personal expression, not to reprising conventional roles and expectations. Then I said, "Well, you're right on schedule. Here you are, age forty. What's dying are your instructions, your understanding of self and world, your script, the story you were given by your culture, which you served ably and well. At the same time, you recognize that this is a summons to something larger. The death that is required is not a biological death. It is the death of an attachment to a story that no longer is applicable."

YOUR FALSE OR PROVISIONAL SELF

When I began to see many examples of dreams like that, to witness people's experience of being in difficult in-betweens, I realized that's what a "passage" is. In a passage, something has played out, grown exhausted, and then the person is in the very, very difficult in-between. Ancient cultures developed rites of passage with the purpose to hold a person together during these transitions and to provide some sort of mythological, theological, or psychological framework that helped the person reassemble on the other side of that chasm. Sometimes crossing that chasm can take years—not days, hours, or weeks as we might fantasize. There can be years of difficult times of in-betweenness. At the same time, something in us has produced that process. It's how the psyche wishes to grow, to change. It's outliving the old constrictive understandings; it's leaving behind the adaptive for the developmental.

It's like the crustaceous creature that has to shed its shell every year. If it doesn't shed that shell, it will die inside. It's too constrictive to live anymore. But during the time its shell is shed, it's extraordinarily vulnerable and at the mercy of its world. That's what it feels like when we begin to let go of the story that perhaps brought us this far. This kind of passage often happens somewhere around midlife, after a person has been living out their scripts and finding discord still growing within. Further, we should not limit midlife here to midlife chronologically. It often happens in the thirties and early forties for the simple reason that by that time, we have played out our first adulthood scripts. When we leave our parents, we walk into the world. We may think, *I know who I am. I'm not going to make the mistakes of my ancestors. I'm going to choose the right person to marry. I'm going to choose the right career. I'm going to choose the right lifestyle.*

After we've been exercising those choices for some time—ten, twenty, twenty-five years—our strengths and liabilities will have made their appearance in various forms of discordant symptoms. At that point, we've also acquired enough ego consciousness, hopefully, to be able to step back and look at our lives and see what is working and what's not. Talk to a twenty-year-old or a twenty-five-year-old and ask them to engage in a genuine critique of their lives. They're almost incapable of doing it. It's not about intelligence or desire. It's about having enough ego strength on the one hand and, on the other hand, a life history sufficient to have something to really reflect upon. You could imagine a person writing their memoir at age twenty-five, but it's probably not going to be as interesting as the one written by a fifty- or seventy-five-year-old.

I recently was reading about a man who spent his adult life working in an automotive plant in Ohio, and the plant closed. He said, "I don't believe I exist anymore. I mean, this has been my life." I understand that. His role was his story. His role was his life, and it was taken away by economic forces and economic shifts. Hence, as the story goes, his understanding of his entire life is now in question.

Perhaps someone suffers a significant loss—the death of a partner, a divorce, the aging process, or the onset of an illness. There are a thousand precipitating events or circumstances, both outer and inner, that can trigger radical reconsideration of what our life is about: Who am I apart from my roles? Who am I apart from my history? Who am I apart from my stories? Where do I go from here? And in service to what road maps? In service to what stories? Now remember, as we discussed in the previous chapter, we all accumulate stories as we're trying to make sense of the world: Who are you? Who am I? How are we dealing with each other? Is the world safe or unsafe? How do I manage this rather difficult transit we call life? We produce what the British psychiatrist D. W. Winnicott called "the false self." Not false because we're hypocritical; false because it's adaptive rather than rising out of our nature.

Often when the false self, or the provisional self—which again is derived from the internalization of childhood messages or stories—collides with the natural, spontaneous, instinctually grounded self that is wishing for change, then you realize that something else is wishing acknowledgment. Something else, some autonomous force within, has brought you to an accountability.

I remember fully the first dream I had when I started analysis at age thirty-seven in Zurich. It was a typical midlife dream. I had recently visited a medieval castle with my family before starting the studies and analysis. And in the dream, I was a knight standing on the ramparts of the castle, and the castle was under siege. The air was thick with arrows flying toward the castle. In the middle of that dream, I felt genuine anxiety. Would the castle hold? Would those ramparts be strong enough to resist the arrows?

At the same time, I could tell in the distance, at the edge of a forest, there was a presence directing that attack. It was, as best I could discern, a kind of witch-like figure. Now, what's a witch doing in my dream at midlife in Switzerland? Then, the dream ended with a serious sense of anxiety. Will the castle hold? Now, isn't that a classic midlife dream? The dream dramatizes the fact that our stories, our understanding of self and world, have become our castle, our walls, our protections. We had to have them, that's the important thing. Yet something in us can die from those constrictive walls as well. I remember my analyst saying to me, "Well, what we're going to have to do now is lower the drawbridge and walk out and talk to that witch and see why she's so angry with you. What's caused such an uproar?"

I remember thinking two things. First of all, *Are you crazy? She's trying to kill me. That's very dangerous.* Second, I think, *Hey, I've traveled this far. In for penny, in for a pound—let's do it.* So we undertook an active imagination to lower the drawbridge, go out, and meet her. That was the beginning of a long, long dialogue with some part of my own psyche. Of course, I was identified with the ego's position, the *I* in the dream, but all the other forces were aspects of me too. But the *I* seldom sees that. The witch was embodying some aspect of myself that I needed to make friends with, or at least have a better conversation with than I'd had theretofore. So it was a classic midlife dream just like the dream of my client whose favorite relative says to her, "It's time to die." Both of us had the sense that the provisional self, our understanding, was under siege and was threatened.

This kind of process happens to all of us at some time. It doesn't mean that people have to go into therapy. It doesn't mean that they even particularly make it conscious. But it's still going on in the unconscious because it's hard to imagine that one could have stories that would serve to help us both effectively manage the world and also be true to our own souls for many, many decades on this planet with all of its shifting circumstances. So somewhere there's going to be a conflict. Somewhere there's a collision. And this collision is inevitable, though sometimes it remains unconscious. It begins to leak through the floorboards as troubling symptoms. You do "the right things," and they just don't feel rewarding anymore. Or maybe you've achieved your goals and found that they're not satisfying; something else is nagging at you. Or perhaps you find difficulties in your relationships because things within you leak into those relationships, whether it's with children or an intimate partner or even at work. In those moments, you begin to realize something else is pushing from below and refuses to be ignored any longer.

It's at that point that we really have to try to track these symptoms and ask, "All right, where are they coming from?" As I suggested in the last chapter, the symptoms represent the protest and constructive criticism of the psyche. We may not experience it at the time, and we may ask, quite understandably from an ego standpoint: How quickly do I get rid of these? What is the right technique or the right medication?

Instead, we should ask: What is it that is wishing further expression in me? What is neglected or repressed or split off or cut off? What is it that wishes an audience with me? These are not questions that we normally ask of ourselves. We only ask them when our symptoms become intense enough. In my own experience, it was the encounter with the midlife depression. I subsequently came to recognize that a depression of that nature was the psyche's autonomous withdrawal of support and approval from the places where my driving engines, my stories, were placing their investments. Something that was experienced pathologically—that is to say, was felt very painfully and disruptively—was in fact seeking new life, new growth, new development. But it took a while to recognize that.

When we look at these passages in our lives—referred to as the "middle passages" because they're between the adolescent passage and our ultimate passage into aging and mortality (which we'll get to later)—we begin to realize every passage is the death of something and the emergence of something else with an often difficult in-between, a liminal period. (From the Greek word for "threshold.") A threshold is always an invitation to the new, but there's that in-between time, that uncertainty, that's very, very difficult.

Out of these passages three issues must be faced, sooner or later. First of all, we are summoned to keep our appointment with destiny. Second, we are asked to reconstruct our provisional map of Self and world. Third, we are asked to track the numinous.

FATE VERSUS DESTINY

Let's look at the first of these three ideas: to keep our appointment with destiny. In the ancient world, there was a significant distinction between fate and destiny. Unfortunately, in our time, we often confuse the two words, making them synonymous, but they're quite different.

Fate represents the circumstances and conditions into which we're thrown, over which we have no control, including our family, our body, our DNA, our time and place, and the formative powerful influences going on around us. The Greek word for fate is *moira*. On the other hand, the ancients understood that each person was given a certain destiny by the gods.

Destiny, or *prooiismus* in Greek, meant what is summoned, what is possible, what is latent within each individual. What was called "tragedy" was not something bad happening. There was a word for that: *catastrophe*. Tragedy rises from the interplay between fate and destiny colluding with the character of the person to produce the texture and contours of a life.

There are certainly times when fate dominates destiny, such as a childhood disease or an illness, or even a death. Anything of that magnitude can be the impact of fate in such proportion that it annihilates or completely dominates destiny. But usually there's some place for human personality to express itself, to play a role. And what is the role of consciousness, of courage, of accountability in the nexus of fate and destiny? How is it we can say fate and destiny are profound force fields of energy flowing through us and through history? Yet, how is it, at the same time, that all philosophies, religions, judicial processes say in the end that we are responsible? We are accountable for how our life plays out? And so we are.

The Greek imagination recognized that there are various elements at work within the function of the human personality: character, hubris, and hamartia.

The first includes our latent tendencies that can be influenced by culture and can be modified but are often innate. In a child, you can often tell something about their core personality, such that when you see them decades later, they're essentially the same person, now housed in a bigger body. The ancient Greeks called that "character." Originally character meant the markings on a slate. Character is the sum of tendencies unique and inherent to each one of us.

Second, they recognized the tendency of the human ego, even then, to inflate itself, to say, *Hey, I know who I am. I'm the boss here. I'm in charge.* So many of the tragic figures of the ancient world were people who arrogated to themselves powers they didn't in fact have, where they crossed those invisible lines drawn by the gods and set in motion consequences that followed. That, we know as hubris. Hubris is psychological inflation. Hubris shows up when I think I know enough to know enough and that I'm making proper choices all the time. Inevitably we don't know enough to know enough about the forces at work within our lives and our choices even as we are required to make important choices on a daily basis.

The third element was something they called "hamartia," which was sometimes translated as "the tragic flaw." However, I refer to it here as "the biased lens." Each of us has a lens through which we see the world. As the German philosopher Immanuel Kant pointed out around 1800, if we wear blue spectacles, we see a blue world. We don't see the world as it is. We see it as our lens allows us to see it. Our stories, our cultural conditioning, our physiology, our emotional life, our typology—all of these things in a sense are different aspects that grind the lens through which we see the world.

All of these things represent, in a sense, distortions in our relationship to both outer and inner reality. Yet we have to make choices based upon those altering lenses. Now you put all that together and we find a very sophisticated psychology, a very sophisticated understanding of how we can set off in the world with the best of intentions heading in one direction and wind up in quite a different place in life.

Sometimes people scratch their head and say, "How did I wind up in this relationship?" Or, "What was I thinking when I chose this career?" Or, "What was at work in that particular vital nexus of decision-making in my life?" Then there are those who never bother to ask those questions and just keep on making the same old mistakes. But for each traveling soul, the summons is to recognize the role fate plays in limiting us and yet to honor destiny seeking to unfold through us. We could say that our common destiny is in service to the Self because it's the transcendent part of us that critiques our adaptations to the world. Understandably, our ego's been trying to make the passage easier for us, but sometimes at the price of violating our purpose and violating our larger calling.

A Dream of the False Self

The wisdom of the ancients affirms that we all have an appointment with destiny. Am I going to somehow show up as myself as best I can under the conditions, external and internal, that life has presented me? Immediately, when we have such encounters, our anxiety management system often turns to regressive, outworn adaptations in the face of the risk of living a larger life.

Carl Jung said once, "We all walk in shoes too small for us," and that rather homey metaphor was his way of saying we necessarily have adaptive, protective patterns and stories, but because of that, they limit our summons from destiny. We all have a kind of phenomenological "reading" of the world, as we have seen. In other words, the world is a grand phenomenon, but our phenomenological reading of it is not so much conscious as it is experiential and highly subjectivized. It's this "reading" that leads to the false self—to the assemblage of behaviors, attitudes, and reflexive responses we use to get our needs met, manage anxieties as best we can, and deal with those existential threats of overwhelment and abandonment, which I mentioned in the prior chapter. All of this produces our archaic provisional sense of self based on the inaccurate disempowered interpretation of self and world the child necessarily has to assemble.

Let me give you another example. A British graduate student, who was living in Zurich studying German language and literature with the intention of becoming an academic back in the UK, was in his late thirties when I saw him. He came with two presenting issues. First was a middle-grade depression that had been with him most of his life that didn't keep him from functioning but certainly took any sense of enjoyment out of life. Second was a difficulty sustaining intimate relationships.

He had a profoundly imaginative dream that illustrated everything. In the dream, he's back in the UK (although the dream was dreamed in Zurich) with his family of origin, and they're going on a vacation. They leave London for the countryside. As they're driving into the countryside, he sees what he called "peasants" at work in the fields. He points out to his parents with a certain gravity in his voice, "You see those people; those are the real people." They drive on. They stop at an inn for lunch. They get back in the car. They drive on, and then it's beginning to get dark as the day wanes.

They reach the end of the road. There's no civilization around them. They get out of the car, and they start walking into the woods. It's getting darker and a little scary. Then in the distance, they see a glow of light and hear some sounds. As they get closer, they perceive sounds of music filtering through the trees. As they get closer still, they find to their surprise, in the middle of this forest, is a large mansion. They walk up to the mansion and then mysteriously, his father says to the dreamer, "This is Keats's house." The graduate student of literature (the dreamer) said, "No, no, it couldn't be Keats's house. He lived in London; he never came out here." Which was factually the case, but they get close to the entrance and sure enough, there is a bronze plaque there that reads "This is Keats's house."

They walk in, and there's a theater-in-the-round presentation happening. Everybody's sitting on the floor instead of in seats. They're motioned to go forward to the front of the audience and sit on the floor, which they do. As they do, he realizes there's a dramatic musical ballet going on. It turns out to be a ballet based on *A Midsummer Night's Dream*. He's enjoying the flow of the music and of the dancers, and then one of the dancers walks over and offers her hand to the dreamer, takes his hand, and pulls him up. He's reluctant, but she pulls him into the circle and invites him to dance.

They start to dance, at which point a telephone rings. As the British say, he's "rung up," and they bring a phone to him in the middle of this presentation; it's all very embarrassing. On the phone is his mother, and it turns out, his mother was left in the bathroom back at the inn that they stopped at for lunch. She got locked in the restroom and is furious, and she insists on his coming back to get her. He's angry because the last thing he wants to do is to leave this performance and this invitation, and yet her demand is unavoidable. The dream ends with a tremendous sense of frustration and duty: "I must go back and take care of her." And that's the end of the dream.

Now stop and ask yourself, *Who would ever make things up like this?* I mean, it's incredibly complicated, full of associations, and so forth. You could probably grasp some of the implications of this dream and also the dreamer's personal associations. You know, we can have dreams about the same images, same story, but they have quite different meanings depending on our associations.

If you dream of your grandmother and I dream of my grandmother, they're different grandmothers, different worlds of associations. They are never quite the same grandmother. Back to the grad student: one of his reasons for studying abroad was to leave that sort of dominating family. The dream puts him back in London, where it all began. In other words, we can run but not hide, and whatever we've left behind stays with us, as we know. In the dream, they leave the world of ego consciousness, the world of the urban life city, and go out into the world of nature and to the increasing presence of nature and the unconscious.

Recall that pronouncement he made, that out there are the "real people." He always felt that there was something constrained and artificial about his life. There's nothing wrong with the life of the mind. It's rich and wonderful.

At the same time, he realized it was partly chosen to exclude other aspects of his personality and the calling toward a more variegated life. Thus, the farmers out in the field were working the earth—working with the Great Mother, so to speak—and in fructifying ways. They were more real than he was. Then they go into the forest. As you know, the forest is one of the primal symbols in dreams and mythology of entering into the world of the unknown, the world of the unconscious. Of course, we remember the first line of Dante's *Inferno*, "In the midway of this our mortal life, I found me in a gloomy wood, astray."[1]

I asked him, "What did it mean that your father makes this very sort of grand pronouncement about this being Keats's house?"

He said, "You know, he wouldn't have known that fact in reality, but in the dream, he knows this is Keats's house."

"So what are your associations? Why would the dream maker call up central casting and ask for John Keats, the nineteenth-century poet?" I asked.

"Well, because Keats's life was so short; he died when he was twenty-five. Keats had such a fragile hold on life. He actually wrote for his epitaph, 'Here lies one whose name was writ in water,' suggesting his evanescent hold on life."

The dreamer felt that about himself, that his purchase on life was very fragile, depending basically on the use of his wits, his mind, to make the connections. "What do you think it means that your father makes this announcement?" I said.

He very quickly said, "Well, he didn't live his life either."

"What was his life about?" I asked.

"Well, his life was always trying to take care of Mother's demands. That was his job," he said.

We can learn a lot from that kind of association because we realize that's exactly what would've been seen by the child as his assignment as well. So they enter the woods and right there in the unconscious is this very grand mansion, suggesting something, again, of the center of the personality, the Self, and how rich and valuable it could be. He's invited to the inner chamber, as it were, and even more, invited to the dance of life. His association with *A Midsummer Night's Dream* was joie de vivre, the joy of life. Here he was invited to the dance of life.

At which point, the old complex rings him up and pulls him out of there. It's almost as if whenever there's a telephone call in a dream, you know there's a complex on the other end calling you away from this moment to an old place, an old value. He's furious, of course, in the dream. But at the same time, the power of that demand is so great he feels as if he has no choice but to leave the dance of life and go back to serve her narcissistic needs, which was his experience as a child.

Then you go back and ask, Why did he come to therapy in the first place? You realize it was because of this depression, because he was always carrying a story that was oppressive to his psyche and to his psychological freedom and development, which of course leads to depression. The story had such power that it continued to pull him away from the possibility of engaging in meaningful relationships. Here are examples of projection and transference again. What he projects onto each of his potential partners is something of the narcissistic dominating power of that old mother complex and the threat that it represents to his well-being. It's natural that he keeps his distance, sabotages it, bailing out as soon as he can. And recall that his second complaint when coming to see me was difficulty in sustaining intimacy in relationships. This is projection and transference at work again in the patterning of adult relationships.

The Path of Enlargement

In the grad student's dream, the psyche was trying to lay out for him in very clear terms both his dilemma and its causal factors. This dream had a large impact upon him because he certainly respected the symbolic life, and he began to realize it was time to question that provisional sense of self, to ask those same questions I mentioned earlier: Who am I apart from that history? What are the agencies within me that are making my choices, especially these repetitive patterns? He began to realize his enemy was not life. His enemy was not other potential partners. It was the power and fear attached to the old mother complex. It was also to recognize the strange paradox of how the assemblage of stories and coping behaviors became the chief obstacle.

That's the thing I learned most in my years of analysis in Zurich many years ago. I've seen it play out time and time again. It's a strange paradox, and it's threatening. It's even demoralizing, but the paradox is basically that "what I've become is now my chief obstacle." It's that which stands in the way of my opening to the real questions and the real summons of the second half of life. Then one has to face the questions: Am I living my life, or the received scripts of someone else? Again, so how would my life be lived differently? What wants to come into the world through me? Then we look at our daily choices; some of them small, some of them are very large, and we ask: Does this choice make me smaller? Or does it make me larger? Does it enlarge me psychologically? Or is it diminishing me?

You may be afraid of the answer, but you already know the answer. If we choose enlargement, it's not ego enlargement, it's not ego aggrandizement, and it's not becoming important or achieved. It's more about the ego's capacity to expand

and to incorporate more complexity, more paradox, in order, ironically, to be a better servant of nature, of nature seeking fuller expression through us. Then we have a kind of daily challenge, a daily mantra, a summons to recognize that our life can't continue to be dominated by fear and our adaptive systems.

Many years ago, when I was writing a book on what matters most (in addition to the obvious responses of work and love and so forth), what came up first on my interior screen was this: It matters most that our life not be governed by fear. We can't avoid fear. Life is difficult, dangerous, and lethal. But the question is: Does fear dominate our life? Does it make our choices for us? The fear management systems that we were obliged to organize have now become shadow governments for us. They run our lives, and it's understandable that taking them on is daunting because we will feel less secure. Perhaps we will feel more agitated, more at risk, more vulnerable, but it's only through living that risk that we can get a larger life. If we're walking in shoes too small, what does it mean to step into larger shoes?

In a book he wrote and published in 1912, *Symbols of Transformation*, Jung notes that every morning we awaken desiring to drown in our own source—that is to say, to fall back into the sleep of childhood unconsciousness. We all contain a regressive, powerful urge to stay asleep even if our body gets up and goes to work. He notes that historically, those inherent tendencies were opposed by what he called those "great psychotherapeutic systems" we call the religions and the rites of passage that provided credos, rites, and sanctions to mobilize libido or psychic energy and are in service to growth in development. He also goes on to say, the spirit of evil—notice his strong language—is negation of the life force by fear. Only boldness, he said, can deliver us from fear. And if the risk is not taken, the meaning of life is violated.

That's pretty clear. In fact, I would go so far as to say, if you write those words down and put them on the bathroom mirror, look at them every day, reflect on them, and internalize them, it'll change your life because you'll start recognizing how many behaviors are fear based and what the alternative may be. What you get from that is a larger life. *The spirit of evil is negation of the life force by fear. Only boldness can deliver us from fear. If the risk is not taken, the meaning of life is violated.* Because then we have to ask ourselves, who or what are we serving when we serve fear and anxiety? When we serve fear or anxiety only, we inevitably will also suffer a neurosis, the psyche's response to its diminishment or neglect.

Neurosis is kind of an ugly term that came from an eighteenth-century physician by the name of William Cullen, who thought of the body as a machine. So our mental sufferings are a result of physiological impairments and wounds of various kinds. What "neurosis" really means is a conflict between the world around us, our own nature trying to express itself, and of alternatively, all of our adaptive systems trying to work these things out. The ego is a nervous creature running back and forth trying to keep the world happy and trying to keep the soul happy. Good luck with that project. Yet as Jung pointed out, the moment of an outbreak of a neurosis is not just a matter of chance; it's usually the moment when a new psychological adjustment, a new adaptation, is demanded. Now that's not really as obscure as it may first appear. Jung is saying that things heat up when change is called for; we start feeling worse when the time comes to move to a new understanding, a new set of choices, a new framework for living our lives.

The first task that we all have to face, whether it's at midlife chronologically or at some later period in our journey, is to try to keep our appointment with destiny. Again, what that means is to become a servant of life. That sometimes means my safety, my security, or my understanding of things is something I've outgrown. Something within me is calling me to something larger.

One of the big sources of conflict in our world today is between those who are terrified and resistant to change and those who can somehow embrace it and move into it. Now, it's easy to talk about embracing change. We might all say so, but when our security or our core understandings is linked to the old, it's not an easy thing to let go.

RECONSTRUCTING OUR PROVISIONAL
MAP OF SELF AND WORLD

The second task in getting to the other side of a passage is essentially the encounter with the therapeutic paradox of midlife, to recognize how each of us in our own way stands as an obstacle. Therefore, we have to reconstruct our provisional map of the world.

Freud talked about therapy being "nacherzieung," which means literally "educating backward" or "reeducating." All of our core stories are provisional understandings of self and world, and when we encounter the insurgency of the Self, it overthrows our ego sovereignty. My own experience was having achieved virtually everything that I set out to achieve in my late twenties and early thirties and then was stricken, as I mentioned, with the midlife depression. How could I account for that when my goals were met?

We have to acknowledge the other forces at work. Already there are losses that we have to account for—losses in relationship, youthful fantasies, hopes, projects, changes in the body. All of these things represent the autonomous process of nature moving forward. Nature's not interested in our comfort.

It's interested in its own fulfillment, its own fruition. We're forced to recognize the reality of many of our limitations. We're not going to achieve everything that we wished to achieve in life. So we have to start moving essentially from a kind of idealized, imaginative, heroic world to a world of realism.

We also begin to recognize that even our closest relationships, at best, can only be partial. We learn to see how deeply buried the "intrapsychic imago" is within us, or the image of the beloved other, what I call "the magical other"— the idea that there's a person who's going to make our life work for us, who's going to understand us, meet our needs, and if we're really, really lucky, help us avoid having to grow up and deal with all that stuff ourselves. So, usually by midlife and later, that expectation has taken a beating. Thus begins the difficult task of relinquishing the fantasy of the magical other.

Some relationships are obviously better than others. In the real world, we all have to make decisions about that. But on the other hand, we slowly begin to discern that nobody out there is going to fix our life for us. That's our job. We may do an imperfect job of it, but we can't avoid the daily summons to that work. This again is the erosion of the projections that we all have as we go out into the world. In other words, as I mentioned in the prior chapter, a projection is an unconscious mechanism.

There are typically five stages of a projection. First, our psyche is triggered and some energy leaves us, goes out into the world, falls on a particular person, a career, an institution, or our children—something that's capable of holding, at least for a while, that projection. We start responding to that other as if it's the reality, not understanding that we're in some way encountering disowned aspects of ourselves.

Second, because the other is "other," there's invariably a kind of discrepancy that we begin to recognize. It's almost as if we put on the wrong pair of glasses. The world is somehow blurry instead of clear. So we may think of the other, *What's wrong with you? You've changed. You're not the person I thought you were. You're different.* Or, *Why is it that this wonderful career or expectation that I have is not working in the way in which I wanted it to?*

That's the experience of cognitive dissonance. Because it's still unconscious, we still assume the problem is out there, and that can lead to the problem of power. In this third stage, people frequently fall into controlling behaviors or passive-aggressive behaviors in their intimate relationships, or they start tinkering with this or that in the outer world, thinking, *If I can just find the right combination of this or that, it'll all still work out.* Unwittingly, the power complex is trying to ratify and reinforce the expectation, the hidden agenda of the projection in the first place.

The fourth stage is when the projection wears away because the otherness of the other wears through it and collapses the energy that's involved. That collapse can lead to confusion or dismay or anger. Often people will wind up blaming each other. "I was counting on you for this or that. You really let me down." Or, "You failed," or something like that. We've all had that experience of burnout where we invest in a relationship or invest in a career or invest in some project or even a hobby and suddenly it no longer has any feedback. It has no reciprocity to it. You realize the projection has failed, but you may not know that existed as a projection at all. You may still be swimming in that unconscious mechanism and thus you're likely to just renew that projection on another person, in another situation, in another hobby, in another distraction, or whatever. Even serial failures or disappointments may fail to produce insight that says, *All of this is about what is unaddressed in you, not in the other you now judge.*

The fifth stage, if it's going to happen at all, is where you have to own this hidden agenda: *Oh, that energy has come back to me. What am I going to do? How am I responsible for that now? What did I put out on you? Or what did I put out on that other that has now come back to me and I'm accountable for it?* To give you an obvious example, think of the famous empty-nest syndrome. Even though I knew it was coming, when my daughter, having completed graduate school, drove through town en route to her own career in a distant city, knowing that my heart drove away with her, I still experienced a reactive depression. So I had to play that little trick that therapists can sometimes play on themselves, and it helps, so I pass it on to you. You can ask yourself, *What would I say to someone else who brought this problem to me?*

What I said to myself was, *Well, that was energy well spent. Look at the result. She's a wonderful young adult. She's living her journey. How much better it is than if she were staying home, frightened, afraid, stuck, and here forever. Now when that energy's come back to you, what are you going to do with it?* And while she was driving, I thought, *Maybe it's time for another child.* So, I started writing a book. That book became *The Middle Passage*, which came out a number of years ago. What I was recognizing there was *I'm experiencing this myself—the erosion of a projection and the recognition that that energy has now come back to me, and I'm accountable for it. What will I do with it?* So, the creative process moved from one arena to another, and a new chapter ensued.

Another question that has to follow that is: *Now that I know what the ego wants, and now that I think I know what the complexes or the old stories want, what does the psyche want from me? What is the soul asking of me, rather than what those old archaic messages want?* When we think it through in this way, we begin to realize that the reconfiguration of our plan and the reconfiguration of our worldview are how life grows and changes, how we mature, and that different understandings and maps of the world are appropriate for not only moving through different terrain but also different stages of our journey.

One of the saddest and most pathetic things to observe is when people are stuck in a previous role, stuck in a previous map, and hanging on to it at all costs. I've seen that in many social figures, for example, who continue to want to be the belle of the ball or the star of some kind, and clinging to that in later years becomes a very sad story. But it's because they haven't been able to see they are more than their role, their persona, their script. Our understanding of ourselves in the context of the world is only a map. If I gave you a map of Arizona and you're in Texas, you may say, "What's your problem? This map doesn't work anymore. Give me a map of where I really am functioning." But if a person clings to the old map, you realize how they are colluding with their own destruction, with their own sabotage of the summons to show up.

ENCOUNTERING THE NUMINOUS

To move through the in-between time, through a "middle passage," after keeping our appointment with destiny and reconstructing our provisional map of Self in the world, a third task is to follow the numinous. This project is about finding apertures into the mystery of life, of our place and role in it. As Jung pointed out, our life is a brief journey, a pause, between two great mysteries. We ourselves are a mystery. And that invites us to consider the numinous. The word *numinous* comes from a Latin verb that means to beckon or be summoned. So we don't create numinosity. It's something that calls us, that speaks to us, that catalyzes an autonomous response within us.

There's a very interesting poem by the Prague-born poet Rainer Maria Rilke titled "Archaic Torso of Apollo." The speaker of the poem is looking at an ancient statue of the God Apollo that has survived the centuries. It is stone, inert matter, but somehow the human spirit entered that stone and brought it something numinous, made stone live. The inert matter is nonetheless living matter, if you will. As the speaker is standing in front of the statue, he experiences some encounter with a numinous presence.

Now if you and I go to an art museum, for example, you might be drawn to one particular painting, and I'm drawn to another one. Something reminds you of childhood, something brings you to tears, or something enlivens your understanding of the world. You're touched by that, and someone else can pass by and not be touched by it. So, as the speaker is looking at this ancient statue and is describing it in great detail, he realizes metaphorically there's something in the statue that's looking at him. There's something confronting him. There's a line in the poem that says, "Nothing here does not see you." And then the poem breaks off into an elliptical pause and then concludes with a kind of non sequitur. It says simply, "You must change your life."[2]

I remember running into that poem as an undergraduate and finding it interesting but puzzling. I didn't get it. I understood that he was encountering some large presence and the presence was encountering him, and he had to change his life. I sort of got that, but I didn't get the full emotional impact of "You must change your life." Years later, of course, I knew full well what that meant.

The speaker of the poem is now confronted by looking at this large imaginative work that has transcended the ravages of time and is being challenged. He's summoned in his smallness to something else. He's called to vocation, vocatus—called out of routine and ordinary life by the numinous. And so we are all, from time to time, called by the numinous. And whatever the numinous is, it's that which opens a window to us. It helps us connect, transcend, transform ordinary life into something that has value and meaning.

The way I put it is this: When the mysterious source of things, the numinous, is not experienced as a living, felt force field of energy, we internalize our need for that in somatic disorders or it leaks into the world through our projections or psychopathologies. Or more commonly, we will be captivated or owned by our projection of the need to connect with the numinous through external objects of desire, such as materialism, romance, power, and so forth. In other words, if we don't feel a link, a personal connection, to the numinous, then we will be in some way pathologizing it or looking for it in the external world. That's how we get hooked to fads, to fashions, to obsessions, to popular enthusiasms. When the going gets tough, the tough go shopping. From popular culture, we are admonished: "Fill that empty spot in your life with the new flat-screen TV and your life will work for you." We know how well that works out. So, when we encounter the numinous, we experience mystery that takes us beyond the ordinary into the realm in which growth, enlargement, is obligatory.

Now, I want to give you a couple of personal examples of that mechanism. In the early 1990s I was asked to speak in Stockholm, Sweden, and the first night, our kind host took us to an outdoor restaurant where, at twilight, everybody stood up and listened to an unknown music. I was told it was the Swedish national anthem, and the national flag was lowered. We stood respectfully, and when that happened, a voice came through my head that said to me, "I have come back for you." And that was it.

I didn't tell anybody, of course, but I had to reflect on what that was about. I realized that my ancestors on my maternal side and one on my paternal side had come from Sweden. I had never met any of them. They'd all died long before I had lived. Even my mother had grown up as an orphan because her father died before she knew him. Her father, Gustav Lindgren, was a Swedish immigrant. But there was no mention of Sweden in our life. My mother didn't know the difference between Sweden and Switzerland. But somehow, in that moment, I had this ancestral voice ripple through me. When my ancestors left their homelands at the end of the nineteenth century, it was forever, and they could never go back. So, these many years later, their grandchild unwittingly was the carrier of some kind of impulse to return on their behalf. As I drove through Sweden for the first time in this ancestral land, I had other experiences that I can't account for. I would only call them déjà vu experiences. The foreign was strangely familiar.

To this day, I can't account for that feeling, but it was an ancestral link to people I'd never met and with whom I had no acquaintance whatsoever. But I see that as an example of the numinous—some force, some power at work, that we need to respect. You respect it by allowing it to stay a mystery and by taking seriously any change of attitude or values that rise from that transformation of the ordinary into the realm of mystery.

Let me give you another example, which I've written about elsewhere. Many years ago, my family lived near Atlantic City, near the casinos, and we did not visit the casinos because there was no point in giving whatever money we had to strangers, which is what basically happens at casinos. But someone gave us free tickets to a show and dinner, and we accepted them. That was the big mistake, and the forgetting, of course, that there's no such thing as a free lunch. We had a meal with about eight hundred other strangers. Afterward, there was a variety show with singers, magicians, performers of various kinds, and comedians. It was entertaining. Then two acrobats came out and asked for a volunteer from the audience.

Of course, no one would volunteer. So they went into the audience and pulled this guy up from the crowd, reluctantly, onto the stage. Then, suddenly, there I am on the stage looking at eight hundred total strangers. It would be easy enough to say I had stage fright, but I don't think it was that. It was just a weird, strange, dreamlike atmosphere. I remember thinking, *There is no such thing as a free lunch. Here's where you get to pay for it. Why did you come? What is this that's happening?* The fellow put a microphone in my face and said, "What's your name?" And I told him. "Where's your home?" Long pause. And I thought, *Now, there is a fascinating question. Where's my home? Now. Where is your home,*

home . . . Home is not just where you live. Home is a psychospiritual place, isn't it? And I thought, *What a fascinating question.*

Now, mind you, this is milliseconds in front of a live mic, in front of eight hundred half-drunk people who couldn't care less where I lived. But I'm pausing to reflect on this fascinating question. Rather than stage fright, I think it was the surreality of the whole situation that caused me to disassociate and step into that really, really fine question: Where is one's home? Then what happened inside, again in milliseconds, was almost like the roll out of an interior teleprompter of various places we've lived. I wanted to say "Zurich," which was a place I lived for five or six years, but it was not so much the place as it was a process of coming home to oneself. It was a psychological reconnection, as I've already described. But then I thought, *No, no, that's a metaphor. It would not make any sense if I said that to the group here.*

All the while, people were laughing at me, with good reason, and finally he said, "Oh, I ask you too tough a question, right?" At which point, it broke the spell and I was able to mention where we lived at the time. Then we went on and played out their act, and I almost got killed in it. Literally. It was physically dangerous. To this day I can't conceive of how the casinos could allow an act that was so potentially injurious to an audience member.

As we were walking out, people were nudging me and saying, "You're part of the act, right? I mean, nobody could be as dumb as you were without being a stooge who works for this group."

"No, trust me. We just came for the free meal," I said.

In the days and weeks and months later, as I reflected on that question, I thought how revelatory that was, the surreality of the occasion threw me into the unconscious. In that, I was able to ponder in a new way such an important question in one's life. In other words, it wasn't a grand revelation but a revelation still to see the importance of my own analysis in a new way; that what Zurich was, was not the city but a symbol of the process. It led me to embrace the paradox that our home is our spiritual, psychological journey of maturation. In short, our journey is our home, and when we recognize that, we can be home anywhere as long as we're present to our journey.

TRACKING THE MOVEMENT OF THE GODS

Another thing that bears some reflection is the question of belonging. We all want at some level to belong. Often in our fractionated world, a world in which we have increased electronic connectivity, we also have more atomization, and we have more and more isolation. I've read studies that indicate that approximately 40 percent of the entire population of our major cities feels profoundly alone and lonely. (A couple of nations, Japan and the UK, have created ministries of loneliness at the cabinet level to cope with the phenomenon.) One of the things that's happened through this technological revolution that brings the world into our room but also removes us from the world into our room, is the loss of community.

Perhaps you recognize that you may feel separated from many of the values of your time and place. You may feel that you don't fit in, and maybe this book will help you realize you don't have to fit in. You're here to live your journey, which is by definition a separate one, a different one, but we do belong to a community of exiles. We don't run for office. We don't exercise a lot of social power out there, but there are more people like you than you would imagine. You're not as alone as you imagine. I've had the privilege of working with many such individuals. I've met so many on the road through the years, and the community of exiles are those people who somehow are hearing the different drumbeat of their own souls and marching to a different tune. They may, at times, fault themselves. They're not superior to anyone; they're not claiming to be. They're not especially enlightened or gifted, but what they're trying to do is live an honest relationship to their own sense of personal truth. Knowing that that's an ongoing process, they're forever sorting and sifting and growing and learning and having to recalibrate.

Those recalibrations are what bring us new and exciting ventures because, in the end, our task really is to recognize, as Jung suggested, that we live in the mystery. We swim in the mystery, and we have to track the movement of Divinity through the tangible world, to try to track the role of the unconscious powers—which by definition is something we don't know—to see them as they manifest in our dreams, our bodies, our patterns; and to realize we are carriers, humble carriers of the life force that has little interest in our comfort or certainties.

Each of us, in our separate way, is challenged to cooperate in the creation of our story, to write it perhaps in a more considered consciousness, even knowing that all the time, someone else, various accumulated spectral presences that we carry in our psyches, will be trying to write it for us.

Our enemy is, on the one hand, the recrudescent presence of the past, yet part of the richness is how we draw upon it. There's a deeply coursing connection between the child that we were and the person we've become. If we've forgotten that link, then we have to re-member it and bring its invisible reality into the tangible world, knowing that our real enemies in this world are not out there. They're intrapsychic. Remember, Jung pointed out that every morning we awaken, half desiring to drown in our own source, to remain in the sleep of childhood, to remain unconscious. The way I put it, years ago, in *The Middle Passage* was there are two grinning gremlins at the foot of our bed every morning; no matter what we did yesterday or this morning, they are there; and they'll be there tomorrow. One is called fear, and one is called lethargy. Each one wants to nibble our toes. If we give them that much, they'll want the rest of us.

Fear says, *Life is too much. It's too big. You can't manage that. You're not up to that. Hide out, hang out, stay away. It's better that way.*

Lethargy says, *Chill out, cool off, have a bonbon, turn on the telly. Tomorrow's another day.*

Both are the enemies of life. All we have to oppose them is found in our awareness, our courage, and our consistency. Fear is understandable. Life is difficult and lethal. Yet for fear to call the shots is to live a diminished, cowering life. Lethargy is related to one of the four rivers of classical hell, Lethe: if you drink of the waters of Lethe, you forget. What do you forget? You forget your journey. You forget your reason for being here. You forget to show up.

So as I reflect on my own journey—and I'm constantly reflecting on it—the search for the invisible in the visible world has been the most consistent thread in my life. I thought about it as a child. I thought about it as a young adult. I wouldn't have languaged it that way, but it was what made life most interesting to me. Part of it was in considering the cosmos. Part of it was in looking into the dynamics of relationships. Part of it was through self-exploration and the explorations of nature. While many times frustrating or disappointing or even wounding, that consistent search has also brought unexpected blessings and a greater acquaintance with many obscure presences along the way, all of them worthy and demanding respect and remembrance. Because in the end, having a more interesting life, a life that disturbs our complacency, a life that pulls us out of the comfortable and thereby demands a larger spiritual engagement than we plan or feels comfortable, is what matters most to us.

Those old, adaptive stories, as I hope you appreciate by now that we each had to have, also become imprisoning forces. Those adaptations, those acknowledgments of the powers of the world, were necessary in managing the limitations that show up repeatedly in our life. In the end, to have been here, to have shown up as best we could, to have wrestled with these larger questions, to have kept the mystery before us, and to have joyfully accepted being defeated by ever larger things is why we're here.

That line "to be continuously defeated by ever larger things" is in a poem by Rilke titled "The Man Watching."[3] I've always been drawn to that line because my youthful ego would've said, "What's this defeat business? I want to be a winner. I want to triumph over these things." But I realized that what he was intimating was if I'm being continuously defeated by ever larger things, then I'm growing, I'm developing, I'm exploring the mystery, and it gets more and more interesting.

Being defeated by ever larger things is probably the single best way to keep our appointment with destiny. To have taken our journey through this dark, bitter, luminous, wondrous universe, to risk being who we really are, is finally why we are here. Rather than inflating the ego, this journey repositions defeat into proper proportion and, most importantly, serves the wonder of our being here in the first place.

3

Shadow Encounters in
Personal and Public Life

I n this chapter, we're going to consider encounters with the shadow in personal and communal life. The shadow is one of the most problematic and perplexing aspects of Jungian psychology and the world we all live in.

The shadow is not defined as "that which is evil." The shadow represents that within myself or within my organization (such as a religious or educational organization, or even a nation or state) that, when brought to consciousness, I find troubling, problematic, threatening, or perhaps contradictory to my professed values. Certainly evil would be included in that category, but the shadow often has to do more with our resistance to aspects of our own psychological reality. It's something that makes the ego consciousness uncomfortable, and we would prefer not to have to deal with it.

OUR SMALL ADAPTIVE LIVES

Let's imagine that you heard rustling in your basement. Would you really want to go downstairs and find out what that was about? Would you go down there and encounter aspects of the world, and maybe aspects of yourself, that you found troubling and problematic? What if, when you emerged from the basement, you knew more about yourself than you knew before you went down? What if you found out about aspects you didn't like or you didn't really want to know about yourself? That's the shadow metaphor. That's the trope that the American poet Maxine Kumin explores in the poem "Woodchucks" when she talks about how some critters had wound up in her basement. She did all the stuff that most people would normally do, like close off points of entry and so forth and even put down some poison for them. But they turn up anyway, and they have an insidious capacity to show up in spite of her efforts.

After a while, she begins to fall into some troubled rationalizations. They began eating some of her vegetables, and that is when things got personal and the shadow began to make its presence known. She calls herself a "lapsed pacifist fallen from grace puffed with Darwinian pieties for the killing,"[1] and after a while, she is down there with her rifle shooting away. By calling herself a lapsed pacifist, she's saying, *I have these professed high-minded and well-intended values, and I fall from my values from time to time.* Perhaps Darwinian pieties are evoked when we need to justify the survival of the fittest. Surely, she imagines, we're "fitter" than those woodchucks.

She winds up waiting down there every day, until finally she's gotten rid of all them except one "old wily fellow." After a while, he's taken up residence in her psyche. He haunts her, and she finds herself dreaming about him. By now, she is possessed by her righteousness, and she invokes even the Holocaust in her posture of moral justification for violence. In that moment, she is possessed by the shadow—the ready capacity to legitimize any methods if they serve her particular needs.

None of us wishes to encounter this huge lacuna between our professions of piety—or at least our good intentions—and this other energy that serves self-interest. But strangely enough, life seems to conspire at times for us to run into the places in our psyches that we prefer not to visit or acknowledge. One of the characteristics of the power of complexes and protective stories, as we've also discussed in prior chapters, is the ready capacity to find rationalizations to justify them.

Kumin's character said that she intends moral and humane values, at least most of the time. The power of the shadow and our hidden agendas makes it easy to slip into contradictions, which then have to be legitimized in some way. These rationalizations allow us to hold on to our preferred sense of self even while indulging in acts that contradict what we say we believe or intend. "Woodchucks" is a wonderful poem of self-discovery, and it embodies the shadow in an understandable metaphoric form. The fact is, we're always running into our shadow whether we're aware of it or not. So, from time to time, we have to ask ourselves, *What psychic rodents of dark design are bumping around in our basements?*

The shadow was one of Jung's richest concepts and is often misunderstood as synonymous with evil. Naturally, people want to disown any evil in them. I've had people announce that they had no shadow, which told me quickly that they had no understanding of what the shadow is. Paradoxically, our biggest shadow issue is not that we are evil (though sometimes evil slips into the world through us, with or without our intention) but that we live small adaptive lives. In a previous chapter, I cited Jung's homey metaphor that we all walk in shoes too small for us. Why is that? Because the intimidating powers of life are so huge and we are so small. So we are, in some way, easily shadow-driven in the sense of living small lives. Our recurrent denial of the summons to a larger life is probably our biggest shadow issue of all.

WE ARE THE CARRIERS OF THE HUMAN PROJECT

We can't avoid having shadows. Our ego is formed like an archipelago rising out of the primal waters. We don't have an ego when we're born. It slowly assembles through the accretion of shards of experience, often shards of traumatic experience—the me and the not-me, the I and the other, which rise out of the trauma of being split off from our mother's body. It forms slowly, not unlike a tidal pool where fragments adhere to each other and form a provisional rock-like substance, even as an atoll in the ocean that could easily be overwhelmed by that ocean. I often think of the ego as a tiny wafer floating on a large iridescent ocean, arrogating to itself powers it doesn't have.

We need our ego for intentionality, for moral choice, for consistency, for developmental agendas, for producing continuity between one day and the next day in our lives. In that regard, the ego's a functional complex—what Jung called the "central complex of consciousness." But the problem is when it presumes its sovereignty. Of course, in the search for its sovereignty and its security, the ego will typically privilege its own position and split off any discordant values, repress them, or project them onto others: if I don't like something in myself, I can always see it in you.

Remember the words of Jesus: We "can see the speck in our neighbor's eye but not the log in our own." Well, that's acknowledging the shadow. The shadow is often formed as a result of our defenses against what brings us anxiety. What brings us anxiety typically is change, ambiguity, and ambivalence. The ego prefers security, clarity, certainty, and control. So whatever threatens that control is bound to produce an ambivalence that can often lead to shunting that content or that issue off into the unconscious.

Of course, we all need socialization, the progressive integration into the social structure and relationships of our time and place. Every child also needs to be brought into the social contract—an awareness of oughts and shoulds. It's not a huge burden on my psychic integrity for me to stop at stop signs because I'm counting on my neighbor to do the same. At the same time, our socialization usually begins to weigh heavily on the spontaneous nature of the child, and we develop inhibitory fears of punishment and guilt. Often guilt rises not because we've done something wrong; it's often felt as *Who I am is wrong*. It's really a form of anxiety. So we learn to feel guilty.

There are several books that explore the conundrum of why we feel guilty when we say no. Well, that isn't about guilt; it is about the power that fear plays in the formation of protective systems. So inevitably we relegate portions of our daily reality into the shadow world and grow deeply invested in excluding these realities from the conduct of our conscious life. Therefore, the shadow has a certain autonomy because whatever we're not paying attention to or is operating unconsciously is going to play an even larger role in our life than we can even imagine.

Probably the simplest thing that Jung ever said about the shadow was simply that it is what we do not wish to be. He recognized that we all have shadows because we are the carriers of the human project. Why should I assume that I am exempt from the human project? In me, all the values that I wish to disown are part of human nature, and I am but the local iteration of human nature.

There's even something that we could call "the positive shadow." We all developed the false self, the adaptive fitting-in strategies and the protective stories that help us manage, but then we push them into the underground into the unconscious. These include many of our best capacities—our spontaneity and enthusiasm, for example. Ask yourself where the spontaneous, joyous, loving child within you went. Creativity is another example. Over time, we become creatures of practice, of rote design, of reflexive response. What happened to our childlike creativity? We are creatures of passion. We have strong feelings, strong desires, and we want to go live them. But they often get buried under the rubble of adaptations and the weight of collective expectations.

In his *Notes from Underground*, the nineteenth-century Russian novelist Fyodor Dostoevsky wrote in 1864 that the chief freedom of a human being is the capacity to stick our tongue out at the world—such a perverse gesture meaning I am different, not in an adolescent way but in a mature way that says *I am a separate individual, a separate incarnation of our collective journey*. The positive shadow can be those aspects of our own personality that are in fact redemptive in character, creative, developmental, contributory, and serving a life force. Yet they are often experienced as dangerous, or we fear their enactment will take us out on the end of that branch and we will be out there by ourselves.

The twentieth-century poet and playwright T. S. Eliot mentions in "The Family Reunion" that in a world of fugitives, the person going the right direction will appear to be running away. Well, that's shadow too. So, again, don't think of the shadow as synonymous with evil. When we talk about shadow, we're often talking about aspects of the human nature, such as sexuality, greed, violence, and so forth, that are threats to the common security, to the common order, or to the disruption of daily life. No one is suggesting they be lived out in a reckless or unthoughtful way. We do live in a world with a legitimate social claim upon us. On the other hand, what happens in the deformation of sexuality, the channeling of natural energy into guilt or addictive behaviors? What good works flow from the suppression of our strong feeling life? Where does that natural energy go when it has been dislocated from the natural expression of the soul?

PERSONAL VERSUS THE COLLECTIVE SHADOW

When we think about the shadow, we differentiate the personal from the collective shadow. The personal shadow obviously is tied to the life of the individual and whatever material or agendas they have repressed in the course of their development. The shadow is what I don't know about myself or do not wish to know. One of the things we don't want to acknowledge about ourselves is that often our life is governed by shadow governments, by the power of certain autonomous complexes or clusters of our history. We have them because we have history. We can't avoid complexes, motives, and agendas contradictory to ego's professions. As Jung pointed out, there's a big difference between having a complex and a complex having us. We have complexes and stories that are laden with energy because we've had life experience. The personal shadow is that in myself that I'd prefer not to acknowledge because it's contradictory to my intended values.

There's also the collective shadow. I used to live near and work in the city of Philadelphia. One of the sayings in Philadelphia by Philadelphians about their Quaker ancestors was "They came to Philadelphia to do good and did quite well indeed, thank you." Philly street wit and wisdom sees shadow work in those sober builders of their city, especially when they could turn a tidy profit from their acts of good intention. So there are often mixed motives in our personal operations that contribute to the collective shadow. When we think about the collective shadow, we have to look at how organizations evolve and function. I recall as a child my parents truly believed that they could expect integrity and the truth from their government, their religious organizations, their cultural leaders, and so forth. They meant well and assumed everyone else did.

A lot has happened over the last few decades to undermine that confidence. But most of us today, when we think about government, we think about cynical misuses of power and greed, and sinister motives. We recognize that all institutions are challenged in terms of their moral authority, whether it's a university or religious organization, because the stories are less likely to be repressed today than they were in the past. When we think about the collective shadow, the first cliché example everyone thinks about, of course, is Nazi Germany, and for many good reasons. There we see state-sponsored terrorism and the corruption and violation of a nation's values, especially a nation that produced so many great humanistic, artistic, and scientific contributions to the furthering of humankind.

In 1933, students in central Frankfurt, Germany, got caught up in the shadow and enthusiastically created bonfires for the books of thinkers, poets, and artists whose differing values posed an obstacle to the new order. There's a plaque there marking the occasion that features a sentence from the nineteenth-century poet Heinrich Heine, who said prophetically, "Where you burn books, you burn people in the end."[2] So whenever you have a government that's allied against speaking the truth, honoring its great traditions, and flies in the face of scientific and educational reality, you have a government and a system that are in trouble. Then truth is subverted, science and education devalued, and reality distorted to fit the contours of the shadow power complex. We may see many such similar devaluations of science and education in our contemporary culture.

Those of us who were born in America were raised with the constant din in popular media and in our history classes of the US wearing the white hat in history's melodrama. We were the good guy who rescued the world from poverty and barbarism and so forth. For sure, this country has done many, many wonderful things. We are a nation of immigrants. My ancestors are immigrants, probably yours as well. Even Indigenous populations arrived here from somewhere else. But then what we all still have to come to terms with is the price of that Western movement, what was rationalized as "manifest destiny." There's the perfect example of the intellectual rationalization of a shadow motive—manifest destiny. Remember Maxine Kumin who wrote about being puffed with Darwinian pieties. In other words, Darwin said it's about the survival of the fittest, and we're the fittest, or so we are convinced.

Manifest destiny. It's our manifest destiny to destroy Indigenous populations and to produce disease and genocide. What "destiny" is served by a country that has been based upon and continues to suffer the evil of racism, that imported hundreds of thousands of people here as slaves, and that essentially engaged in genocide against Indigenous populations? That's hardly a country that can claim to be free of a very large shadow. After 9/11, I remember a lot of people said, "Oh, what did they do to us? We're nice people; we bring good everywhere. Why don't they like us?" Well, one of the things we might do, if one can bear it, is talk to other people around the world and ask: How is it you experience America? Are we the good guys? How do you feel about how our businesses operate, our military, our government policies? How does that look from your perspective? Don't be polite—what is your experience of us? Then you might begin to hear a different story.

The ragged edges of shadow are often finessed through abstractions and euphemisms like "manifest destiny." In the nineteenth century, for example, when a burgeoning population was taking over this continent, there were two flourishing literary groups. One was the transcendentalists, who talked mostly about the numinous powers of nature, which were present and indeed powerful. On the other hand were the works that we still read today and still have relevance to us. Much of classical American literature explored the dark side of the American story—the writings of Nathaniel Hawthorne, Herman Melville, Edgar Allan Poe, Mark Twain, and others.

All of Hawthorne's stories and novels in some way are directly linked to the shadow, not just *The Scarlet Letter* but many of his short stories too. Same with Ahab's pursuit of the great white whale. The whale was just nature naturing. Where was the evil to be found: in that driven, monomaniacal Captain Ahab or a natural creature doing its natural thing? And of course, Poe speaks for himself in his preoccupation with the shadow. Mark Twain used comedy to eviscerate the pretensions in pieties of his era. I came across a quote of his once that said something along the lines of "Please, please don't let my mother know that I'm interested in politics. I tell her, I play the piano at a local house of prostitution." Using comic insights, Twain saw and revealed so much about the workings of shadow agendas in his time. The literature that survives and continues to speak to us is the literature of the shadow, not the literature of transcendence of it. We may think we can run from the shadow but it travels where we travel.

THE SHADOW MODALITIES

There are different venues, different modalities in which the shadow manifests. First and by far most commonly, it stays unconscious. This is when I don't know what motive I'm in service to at any given moment: Why did I do that? I don't know. Maybe if I start probing, I might find a rationalization to legitimize it. Well, we rationalize, slip-slide away, "I just said that because you said this" or "I only did that because such and such was true." My willingness to confront my own shadow aspect has dissolved and slipped away, but the unconscious is constantly spilling into the world.

There are shadow invasions in the world continuously, which lead to moral dilemmas. In his Letter to the Romans, Paul the apostle wrote, "Though I know the good, I do not do the good" (7:19). Why? His answer was a Greek word, *akrasia*, which could be translated as "a dilatory or insufficient will." In other words, "I haven't willed the good enough, and when I will it enough, it will happen." The problem with that is Paul didn't know very much about the unconscious. We now know that in a certain way, the shadow has a will of its own too. It looks for places to spill into the world, and no amount of moral exhortation will always make people do the good thing, whatever the good thing might be, because of that autonomy of the shadow.

The reason for that paradox is simple. The human psyche is not a single unitary thing, as our ego would like to presume. It's diverse and divided—always divided. It's essentially the delusion of the ego that this aggregate of splinter selves and energy systems is under our control, contained within the purview of consciousness, serving our noble intentions. But those splinter selves are essentially fractal energy systems and have the power to oppose our conscious intention at any given moment. Another way of putting this is that certain parts of ourselves haven't been introduced to other parts, and if they have, they may not be getting along very well.

The first modality of the shadow is it remains unconscious, and therefore maybe our children have to carry it, maybe our partner does, or maybe our society does. Jung repeatedly noted that the greatest burden any child faces is the unlived life of the parent. What he was saying is a parent might have lived a straightforward conventional life, devoted to good work and so forth, but also lived a very narrow constrained life. That child, then, has that as a psychological burden; his or her imagination is constrained by the example provided. They'll either have to serve it, which is most common; spend time trying to compensate for it; or spend a life trying to break free of it. Where the parent is blocked in their task of individuation forms a template, a limit, an exemplum. Individuation is not narcissistic self-indulgence. Quite the contrary, the individuation summons serves the insurgent impulse of nature seeking to enter the world through us. Anything short of serving our deepest spiritual nature typically becomes a shadow issue for any of us.

In the second modality, the shadow shows up as projection. I previously defined projection as an unconscious mechanism whereby my psyche, having been triggered, sends energy into the world, and because it's unconscious, I don't know that happened. So I start seeing elements in the other person, "seeing the splinter in my neighbor's eye." Projection is also a way of distancing oneself from one's own shadow. In other words, I can see someone else's greed. I can say, "Well, that person is ambitious," or "Look at that person, how jealous they are," and we actually take pleasure in that kind of moral superiority. We seldom realize that the other is carrying our own disowned parts. Who among us in a moment like that would stop and say, "Well, perhaps I should also look at my greed; look at my jealousy," or "look at my anger"?

Sometimes you also see projection in its collective form. We see that in scapegoating, for example, and bigotry, the Holocaust and similar "ethnic cleansings." History is full of the shadow projections onto the group of people across that invisible line, those who have an appearance different from ours, or people who worship a God different from ours. Our incapacity to tolerate otherness within ourself means *I'm unable to tolerate the "other" that you embody*. It is easy to disown our problematic issues and see them in you, the other. If I believe the problem is you, something has to be done about that. And that is where human conflict begins. Most of the horror of history has risen from shadow projection. How many times have armies marched off to war singing a hymn that God is on our side? We are righteous because we march against the infidel. Disowning our own shadow and attacking it in others is so much easier than the humbling work of acknowledging our complicity in life's messier side.

The third arena manifests sometimes when we can get caught up in the shadow, identify with it, groove with it. A lot of people go to concerts primarily to get stoned and enjoy being in that altered awareness, an altered space. With the temporary annihilation of individual consciousness, one is relieved of responsibility for one's actions, values, investments of energy. Jung gave a humorous example of a Swiss businessman who came to him. This man, in his own mind, embodied the Swiss collective expectation of rectitude, respectability, and conventional behaviors. But his dreams showed another whole side to his personality. When he realized he had a shadow, it was overwhelming to him. He got so caught up in it that he began to identify with it. Jung said he disappeared with his company's funds and wasn't seen again. In other words, he saw his shadow, was subsumed by it, and was driven by its compelling energies.

Many years ago, I saw a young man who was about to become a ministerial student. When we explored his motivation to attend seminary, one of the things that he identified was he knew it would please his parents. I said, "Well, that's what we call a complex and not necessarily a calling in life. Let's look at that from a different perspective, and oh, by the way, pay attention to your dreams." At his next session, he told of a dream in which he was involved in a conspiracy to bilk the public. It was some kind of confidence scheme that he was waging with another man whom he didn't really know but saw from afar and thought he didn't like him. He took the position of the ego figure, sort of saying, "Look at that man, look how he fooled people, and see how he enjoys doing that."

I said, "But look, your unconscious has put you and this fellow in league with each other, you're coconspirators. This is an aspect of your shadow." At that moment, the scales fell from his eyes, so to speak, and he realized that he really enjoyed the capacity for public speaking, even to be manipulative, and be, if not worshipped, at least adulated in the pulpit. He realized that at some deep level he had a con man within him.

He said something that I never forgot: "Well, I shouldn't go to seminary. I'll have to go to law school, I guess." Well, that doesn't speak well for lawyers, but at least he recognized the shadow. At that moment he was caught up in it. He was a fairly young person, so if he continued to work on recognizing his shadow dimensions, he would find his calling perhaps in working with the soul of himself and with others.

We also recall how an identification with the shadow is what fuels the tourist industry of, say, Las Vegas and New Orleans, for example, to let the good times roll. It brings properly good people from various parts of the country just to have a little taste of temptation, of living a bit more dangerously than one's daily comportment but not too much. While there, they can explore the risqué, overthrow prudence and bet it all, laugh at smutty comedians, and remain anonymous for "what happens in Vegas stays in Vegas." They can get on their planes and fly back the next day and be safe from all of that. But the appeal is there, and a secret identification with the shadow proves compelling. One may sleep all the better knowing that all that tempting stuff is out there, over in that other city, and not in one's soul.

The fourth modality through which the shadow may manifests in our life is by confronting it. Frankly, we usually confront our shadow because we've been forced to: perhaps consequences pile up that we have to deal with. Our children carry out the unfinished business of our life. Someone gets in our face and says, "This is what you did; this is how you hurt me or disappointed me." In those disquieting moments, there's an invitation to assimilate into consciousness more of your shadow.

Jung said repeatedly in his memoir *Memories, Dreams, Reflections*, when he talked about his own process: here's another thing that I found out about myself, and it felt like a defeat. Well, why would it feel like a defeat? It feels like a defeat because the ego is in service to its fantasy of its purity, its sovereignty, and its capacity to lead a conscious, purposeful, shadow-free life. But here we are, tripping over ourselves once again and we are being obliged to consider what forces are at work within us.

To Jung's credit, of course, he continued his explorations of the shadow, and he invited us to consider it in ourselves as well. To assimilate the shadow is really to break its compelling hold on us because, otherwise, nothing is more powerful than when something is working from the unconscious. When it is unconscious, we can't face it because we don't know how it's entering the world through our decisions and behaviors. When we struggle with our choices and their sometimes-troubling consequences and work backward, we often have to recognize the motives that were buried agendas we didn't know were there and entered the world through us.

Jung frequently reminded us that our task in life is not goodness but wholeness. Now I don't know about you, but I never heard anything like that when I was a child. And I wish I had. Like most children, whenever I had what I would consider a shadow thought, fantasy, or hope, I immediately felt awful about it because of the weight of collective expectation to always be "good." When that happened, I believed "goodness" alone is the task; it is what I had to do. Pieces of one's life are pushed aside, projected onto others, or dropped back into the unconscious where they will sooner or later act autonomously. So when Jung said wholeness is a task, we face quite a different story for our lives. He writes profoundly about how we need to explore all aspects of our life, the body, desire, and moral exploration, and not out of a selfish narcissistic agenda. I don't mean to suggest, nor did Jung, an unfettered license to any moral choice; rather, this is about responsibly knowing that all choices lie within me, and I am accountable for their entry into the world—if I'm going to deal with what is wrong in the world, I have to deal with what is wrong in me first.

He also reminded us that we do not become enlightened by imagining figures of light but by making our darkness visible. This is why shadow work is always, always humbling, because we are asked to confront, be accountable for, what our ego would otherwise repudiate. Let me give you a funny example based on an actual event. It looks like a poem, but it's not really.

Marital Bliss

Waking from a dream on a Sunday afternoon
I slung my arm over my wife,
she who once defined relationship as "having one special person to
annoy for a very long time,"
and asked her if she would marry me again.
"Uhum," she said.
And I said, "I thought you would pause longer, reflect, savor the
moment at least, leave me in ambiguity."
And she said, "I was being polite."

Well so much for "Marital Bliss," but she actually did say that, by the way. And there's a special truth to that. Find one special person to annoy for a very long time and guess what? You both get to work on your shadows—two people, two shadows. That can be part of the dialectic gift of a genuine intimate relationship.

Now, so much of this is really contra new age sentimentality. There are many aspects of the new age philosophy that are of importance, like the redemption and reintegration of feminine energies and values, reappreciation of nature, and the balancing of the material world with the spiritual world. But there's also a shadow to everything, because many times, the new age tendencies are to escape and transcend conflict and suffering. Yet it's conflict and suffering that bring us the fullness of life that Jung was talking about. It's the desire to transcend the difficulties and evils of the world without the descent into the underworld that is necessary for all of us at some point. It often includes a search for gurus, people who have figured all this out and who will perhaps lead us at some level, but even better, reach for shortcuts that will help us avoid the shadow. Avoiding the shadow is not something of which we are capable. The fantasy that we can is itself a shadow issue.

But as Jung said, everyone carries a shadow. If the shadow issue becomes conscious, we then have a chance to correct it. But if it is repressed and isolated from consciousness, it never becomes conscious and it continues to undermine our ego intentions. Jung gave a great deal of credit to Sigmund Freud for articulating the darker sides of the personality. In 1905, Freud wrote *The Psychopathology of Everyday Life*, and he noticed how our so-called Freudian slips—our losses of memory, our forgetfulness, and our humor—are often expressions of violence, anger, and sexuality that allow us to disclaim our true intentions. In his follow-up book, *Jokes and Their Relation to the Unconscious*, he alludes to how one can be outrageous in one's jokes, and then if someone objects, we say, "Can't you take a joke?" It's win-win for the shadow.

On the collective level, Freud also wrote *Civilization and Its Discontents* at the height of the Great War where his own son, Martin, was gravely wounded, and he didn't know if he would see him again. Of course, Freud's id, ego, and superego, which everyone's heard about, is very clear. Id is raw nature naturing; the superego imposes the world of oughts, shoulds, and expectations; and the ego is obliged to shuttle back and forth trying to keep everybody happy—an impossible project.

When we think about it, it's impossible to eradicate the shadow because we never gain full consciousness of it. The moment I say I'm virtuous, I'm already enmeshed in hubris and unaware of the possible ramifications that my value choices may be bringing harm to myself and others.

NOTHING HUMAN IS ALIEN TO ME

A number of years ago, after I wrote a book on the subject of the shadow, the publisher arranged forty radio interviews. These forty radio interviews were all jammed in a two-week period, and some of them were short, drive-home-type interview shows. Others were serious PBS interviews where people had actually read the book and thought about it and expressed very thoughtful questions. Of those forty interviews, I would say approximately thirty of them asked me questions about two "scandalous" things that had happened at the time that were occupying the attention of Americans. They asked my opinion about them, often with the kind of smirking tone that said, "Tell us about these crazy people, so we'll know them when we see them, and we'll know what to do with them."

The first one was the story of an astronaut who drove from Houston to Florida to whack the woman who won the affections of her beloved. The question was, "Can't NASA work out tests and ways of catching the crazies and keeping them out of the astronaut program?" I replied, "Think of the psyche as a large mansion. In anyone's mansion, there are many rooms, and in one of those rooms, there's always a terrified frightened child. The choices of others, our own choices, or unforeseen circumstances may suddenly place us in one of those rooms, and we will feel absolute panic. The most rational thing we can do at the moment is reach out in some way to change all of that. Before we judge her, we need to recognize if we were in a position of such psychological extremity, who knows what we might do."

The other issue that was preoccupying the great intelligence of the American people was why a pop singer had shorn her hair in public in an overtly depersonalizing and humiliating way. One person basically asked me, "What's wrong with this crazy person?" I said, "First of all, if that person came to me in therapy, I would say, 'Do you realize what took over there? The Self, with a capital *S*, was seeking to help heal you of something.'" In a sense, her life, a life desired by many teenagers, a life of a celebrity yet a life in which one lives a plastic existence, was imprisoned in the celebrity's image, encapsulated in public projections, and she had no genuine freedom, as we know from movie stars and figures of royalty and so forth.

Such a life is a horrible life, and something took over to break her out of her bubble. If this were a dream, if you deconstructed her popular image, it would be a way of saying, *Look, I'm dying in here. Let me out of here. I need to break out of this bubble I'm in.* I said, "This was something trying to help her to rescue herself." But, I added, "I predict she'll be put into a rehab and will be back out on the road in a very short time." Which is, of course, what has happened.

It was the Russian playwright Anton Chekhov, who once said, one of the surest signs of our own sanity is we'd like to identify which of our neighbors is crazy, and then we'll know to put them in the asylum. That way we disassociate from our own shadow. Remember that the shadow is composed of disassociated material so there is always a motive to see it "out there" rather than within oneself.

Probably the wisest thing ever said about the shadow was uttered by the Roman African playwright Terence, who, a little over two thousand years ago, said, "Nothing human is alien to me."[3] Again, I am the carrier of the whole human project. In each of us then is the liar, the lecturer, the thief, the criminal, the murderer, and shockingly, maybe even the saint as well.

If we are unaware of those energies, then they will inevitably show up somewhere. They'll show up in our compensatory dreams, which we can ignore. They'll show up in our projections. They'll show up in our children and our children's children. These things don't go away. They always go somewhere.

In 1937, Jung gave a series of lectures at Yale University on the shadow. Let me share with you one important paragraph from his lectures.

> Our ordinary psychological life is swarming with projections. You can find them spread out in the newspapers, books, rumors, and ordinary social gossip. All gaps in actual knowledge are still filled with projections. We are still certain we know what other people think or what their true character is. We are convinced that certain people have all the bad qualities we do not know in ourselves. We must be exceedingly careful not to project our own shadow shamelessly. If you can imagine someone brave enough to withdraw these projections, then you get an individual conscious of a pretty thick shadow. Such a person is now shadowed with new problems and conflicts. Such a person has a serious problem for he's now unable to say they do this or that, they are wrong, they must be fought. Such a person knows that whatever is wrong in the world is in himself, and if he only learns to deal with his own shadow, then he's done something real for the world. He's succeeded in removing an infinitesimal part of the unsolved gigantic problems of our day. How can anyone see straight when he does not even see himself and that darkness he carries into all his dealings?[4]

Well, that comment from 1937 is certainly explicable and applicable to our present, terribly split culture in which we see sides lining up based on ideologies and fears. Everybody has compelling fears, and it widens the gap between us.

We live in a culture of fear—fear of the shadow, fear of depth, fear of self-awareness, fear of others, and even fear of the other within ourselves. Such an age would be trivial if it weren't also so lethal. If we can't tolerate the otherness in ourselves, our shadow, how can we tolerate one another? The first place to begin to do this work is by working on our own shadow.

THE OTHERNESS IN OURSELVES

In the remaining sections of this chapter, I'm going to offer you some questions, some exercises, to help you begin to consider and reflect on the question of the personal shadow. These questions are very simple and nonthreatening, and yet you'll see, they begin to stir the pot. They begin the analytic work of bringing things slowly to the surface.

1. Which of your many virtues shows up in your life with reasonable consistency and intention on your part? List two or three.
2. What is the opposite of each of those virtues? List the opposite for each virtue you listed in #1. For example, if in #1 you answered, "I try to be honest." The opposite is dishonesty.
3. Can you identify a specific occasion where the practice of the virtues you listed in #1 brought harm to you or someone else? Using the honesty example, the question is, Where did the practice of your honesty bring harm to you or harm to someone else?
4. On what specific occasions did the opposite of your virtues, as listed in #2 above, turn up in your life? In other words, where did the opposites show up in your life?

On the surface, these are very simple questions, but a couple of things often happen. One is they tend to disorient the ego. The ego says, *Just a moment here. Now, wait a second. I thought I was clear about this or that.* It's a little disorienting to the ego, but that disorientation begins to soften the hard-edged boundaries of the ego, the ones that say that I'm in charge, and I'm accountable here.

Then the ego realizes that none of us is smart enough or wise enough to foresee the consequences of our choices, that somewhere down the line what I thought was right might bring harm to me, my children, or even unknown strangers. Just by being here, sucking oxygen, consuming energy, we bring harm to this world, not because we're bad people but because we're human beings.

When we begin to look at such material in our lives, the ego's resistance begins to soften to the shadow and the ego's fantasy of sovereignty is undermined.

We begin to realize perhaps that the questions of consequences are often so subtle that we can't possibly imagine what they might look like elsewhere. We couldn't possibly begin to imagine that we could foresee all the consequences that follow.

For example, consider some of the great technological breakthroughs of our time. Back in the late 1990s when the internet was just beginning to burgeon, I was giving a talk about the shadow. Someone said, "This invention can bring about world peace because dictators can't control all the information. They must be terrified of other opinions coming into their land." There's certainly truth to that. If I were a dictator, I would try to control means of access to the world of information. But we also know, whether it's factions interfering in our elections or the recruitment of murderous groups of people, that this great advance has been used and quickly exploited to bring about significant harm to this world and a huge shadow invasion.

This is not to say anything against technological revolution. Rather, it's to ask, who are we to always foresee consequences? We can also say wherever there is an advance of some kind, as the ego sees it, you can be sure that the shadow accompanies it. Everywhere we go, when we stop and look behind us, there's the shadow. This is true for all areas of our achievement as well.

Another point to examine vis-à-vis the shadow is the key relationships of your life—domestic relationships, perhaps friend relationships, and even business relationships. Where has the shadow shown up in those relationships, in your patterns of avoidance, of conflict, or of compliance with the pressure of the moment, leading to decisions that were not in your interests or others' best interests?

One of the things we learned early on as children, as I mentioned earlier, is the world's big and I'm not; the world's powerful and I'm not. Sometimes to get along, you go along and avoid conflict and make nice and stay out of harm's way, which is very rational, very adaptive, and quite common. Yet again, power constitutes a shadow government, doesn't it? A shadow from which enormous consequences come. A shadow in which we realize inauthentic life piles up. Though I know the good, I do not do the good. Sometimes to be a person of value, we have to engage in conflict. Sometimes we have to risk not complying with outer pressures if we're going to be creatures of value.

Underneath all of this is really the question: Can I realize where my decisions are really coming from? Because the real shadow agenda may be simply obedience to my old stories, my old protections, which I've rationalized as goodwill, of being necessary under these circumstances. This is the most troubling thing of all: there's always a rationalization to justify everything. When we look at those relationships, we have to realize many times that the shadow manifests in our patterns of avoidance or compliance with the pressure of the moment, rationalized as it may be and leading to consequences that we wouldn't have imagined. The shadow rises out of what were once protections but later prove costly.

SHADOW IN INTIMATE RELATIONSHIPS

The next point to consider in relation to the shadow is the patterns of your intimate relationships, either current or past. What annoys you most about your partner? Where have you encountered those annoyances before? Jung often said that where we grind away most about someone is where that other is carrying our own shadow that we wish to disown within ourselves. We see other people's insecurities or their greed. We see their need for approval and affection. We may feel superior to that, but we have the same motives within ourselves. So if I recognize that sleight of hand as a kind of scapegoating or projection, it allows me to disassociate from that within myself.

The next questions for you to consider are: Where do you repeatedly undermine your interests? Where and when do you shoot yourself in the foot or cause yourself familiar griefs? Where do you avoid risking what you intuit to be your larger Self? Why would you do that?

We know we could say it's because so much of our psychic life—many of our choices—is in service to those primal stories, the stories that help us avoid anxiety and conflict, the deeply rooted behaviors that protect us. But they undermine our legitimate interests, our summons to life, and therefore take us to a familiar place: the same old, same old. The problem there is the role our old stories and their protections play in those shadow governments that run our lives.

Next, ask yourself: *Where am I stuck in my life? Where am I blocked in my development? What fears stand as sentinels to keep me from where I want to go? From where do they derive?* If you use the word *stuck*—"I'm stuck somewhere"—you're already talking about someplace that consciously you both recognize and repudiate. Yet you remain stuck.

At some point, you might have had a thought such as, *If I could so readily identify where I'm stuck, I should be able to get unstuck.* We have New Year's resolutions. Most of us can identify and judge our flaws, but then we stay stuck. What is that about? Well, I can tell you that being stuck always has its protective motive. Remember, we always act "logically" if we understand the emotional premise from which the behavior arises. Where we are stuck are always places where we're defending against some fear, perhaps unconscious but fear nonetheless.

At first, stuckness presents as anxiety, which is free-floating and formless. It's hard to get a handle on anxiety. It's like fog that covers the highway and keeps you from moving forward. You put your hand out and there is nothing there, yet it's enough to stop your car. That's anxiety. But in every anxiety, there're specific fears. We remain stuck in such places because to get unstuck, to push through, we have to face the fear the avoidance seems to spare us. Typical systemic fears include fear of being alone, suffering the judgment of another, or perhaps losing their affection or approval.

The odds of those things actually happening are often minuscule. In most cases, they're not going to happen. And let us not forget the large resilient self that has grown up since those stories got lodged into our system and became definers of who we are and how we are supposed to act. Thus, stuckness is almost always a flight from some accountability to a fear that is not likely to happen but still has a foothold in our psychic economy. In those moments, we find our shadow in the role that fear plays in our diminished life.

Another question for you to consider is: Where do mother and father still govern your life—through repetition, overcompensation, or your special treatment plan? I'm not blaming parents; everybody's a failed parent at some level. The question is, how do we internalize those stories, those oughts, those shoulds, those expectations? Did we serve them and repeat them? In which case, maybe we're not living our journey but someone else's. Are we overcompensating? Are we trying to get away at any cost and still being defined by that determinative other? Or do we have a special treatment plan, such as an addiction to anesthetize or busyness? Where do the archaic presences continue to show up in imitation, flight from, or efforts to heal?

We all know that death does not end relationships. Even when parents pass, many times their influence persists, and I've known people still to feel inhibited, to feel governed by, or to be living in reaction to parental expectations many years after the passing of the person.

Beneath all of that is our understanding of the power of those primal relationships and their messages. The shadow, then, is found in the power of the past, in the power of the story that there wasn't anything we could do except repeat, run from, or try to fix it somehow.

Next, we must consider our flight from our personal authority. I've said before that the biggest task of the second half of life is the recovery of personal authority, to sort through the plethora of voices that we hear at all times from the outer world and from our inner world and try to find our own. As you sort and sift through that inner traffic, ask: Which voices come from the soul, from the Self? Which are from parental imagos, from my culture? How do I know? It's not easy to sort through this complex set of admonitions, but that work is necessary. Only a disciplined inquiry like this offers a chance to recover personal authority.

The next question is: *Where do I refuse to grow up?* When I've asked people this question in workshops or in therapy, no one has ever hesitated. Everybody has a sense of an area where they need to grow up. A way to define that is a place where you know you need to be accountable, yet for reasons you don't know, you're slip-sliding along. Where do you wait for clarity of vision before risking something? While it's important to gather information, often in life we never get total clarity about anything—and we still have to act.

Life is ambiguous, life is difficult, life is risk-filled, and sometimes we have to take the risk and dive into it. Where is it that you're hoping for external solutions? Where are you expecting rescue from someone or even waiting for someone to show up and tell you what your life is about? Remember, you are not expected to follow what I'm suggesting, other than to ask: *Does this speak to my life? Does it make sense of something?* Then find your own path. My path is my path. Yours is yours. Respectfully, we can learn from each other, but don't wait for someone to tell you what your life is about.

Something inside of you knows what it wants, and the rest of you has to be summoned, mobilized to serve that as best you can. Where we refuse to grow up, are waiting for complete clarity and information before making decisions, or are waiting for somebody to show up and tell us what to do is deferred authority. All of that is shadow because it infantilizes our summons to accountability. All of that allows us to avoid stepping into the large summons of the soul. And any life based on avoidance is a scant life.

SHADOW WORK IS DAUNTING AND HUMBLING

As you can see, shadow work is daunting to be sure. It's at best difficult. It's always, always humbling and frequently leads to still more work, but the alternative is far worse. I've often said to people, "This work of psychological growth, this individuation process, doesn't make one feel inflated; quite the contrary. It's a humbling process, daily." It's repeatedly asking, *Where did that come from in me?* And then discovering, *Oh, here's something else I didn't know about myself.* One of Jung's haunting comments is that what we deny inwardly will tend to come to us in the external world and we will call it fate. That's a scary thought, isn't it? What I've denied inwardly can very well be rushing toward me like a train in a tunnel that I'm entering.

When we realize how important this self-examination is, it's the single best thing we can do for our children, our partners, our society. Jung said that sometimes when people undertake this work of personal growth and development, they remove themselves necessarily from the collective, and they feel a sense of guilt doing that. But, he said, this individual journey is a debt that is repaid by returning to your partner, your children, your family, your neighborhood, as a more evolved person. Your gift is to bring something new and different and alive back to the community, your separate piece of the large mosaic that is humanity. That's why this is not isolating work, but it is humbling work for sure. It involves respecting, if not loving, the disrespectful, unlovable parts of all of us.

In 1931, Jung gave a talk to a group of clerics in Alsace-Lorraine, in what is Strasbourg, France, today. He asked, what if you found that the most needful member of your parish, the most troubled member of your parish, the most despicable member of your parish was you—what would you do then? He was saying that his work is humbling but necessary work. None of us is free from its challenge.

Everything I deny is granted a greater degree of autonomy. Everything I project onto the other ultimately comes back to haunt me. Everything I refuse to face remains a part of my presence in this world. Looking at that, working at it as best we can, lifting that off of our partners and others is the single best thing we can do for the world. Frankly, it makes life more interesting, richer than we ever imagined, and better than the best novel that we've ever read.

4

The Seven Deadly Sins Through
a Psychological Lens

To follow up our conversation about the shadow, in this chapter we're going to look at an old-fashioned term that's maybe not so old-fashioned. That's the idea of sin. Perhaps you are aware that originally the Greek word for sin (hamartia) had to do with archery. It meant to miss the mark, implying that one could never fully hit the target all the time, simply because we're finite and fallible. So, we all find ourselves falling short of our intentions from time to time, which invariably, of course, touches on the issue of shadow. So, then, you might ask, why would a person in the modern era, and maybe the postmodern era, be interested in something called sin?

MISSING THE MARK

Our ancestors reflected at great length on the human condition, and the human condition has not changed. We are the same people today as people were earlier. True, there's been some evolution in our brain structure and in our physiology, but by and large our psyches are very similar. Just read the ancient scriptures, the ancient mythologies, the Greek tragedies, the heroic epics, and so forth and you'll find the repetition of the characteristics of human nature showing up over and over. So when we study sin, what we're really looking at is how people have viewed this phenomenon called the human being and the shadow issues that emanate from that species. The inquiry is to consider this through a modern psychological lens and discover what we can learn from it.

There's a story about President Calvin Coolidge, who was noted for being laconic and introverted to the max, going to church one wintry day when his wife was home ill.[1] When he came back to the White House, his wife said, "Well, what happened?"

"Well, the preacher preached," he said.

"And so, what did he talk about?" she asked.

"Sin!"

"Well, what did he say about it?"

"He's against it!"

Thus, that's Calvin Coolidge on the subject.

Remember, sin comes from the idea of not hitting dead center in one's moral aim. Historically in Judaism, it meant to go against a mere 613 commandments. That's quite a few opportunities to miss the mark. In Buddhism, there's very little concept of sin, although it was generally thought that killing people was bad for one's résumé. In Hinduism, of course, humans accumulate karma or consequences, which then follow them through history. A lot of Hinduism aspiration, then, is to try to work off some of the burden of karma from past shortfalls in one's aim.

Then there's Christianity. You probably remember that old maxim that used to be in the primers of so many children: "In Adam's fall, sinned all." That of course refers to the notion of collective sin, a sort of flaw in the human condition as a result of the archetypal violation of divine will in the Genesis story, leading ultimately to redemption through good works and right effort, and eventually the redemptive sacrifice of Christ.

Just in case you haven't gotten the full complement of sins recently, let me remind you of how our ancestors thought of them: gluttony, lust, wrath, pride, envy, greed, and sloth. Let's look at each one from a traditional perspective as well as from a modern psychological perspective.

THE SIN OF GLUTTONY

We'll start with gluttony. You may have noticed about us, about humans, that we hunger—we always hunger. And for what do we hunger? What feeds us? What nurtures us, really? What abides? Those are unspoken questions that are haunting our culture. As Augustine of Hippo wrote in his *Confessions*, "Our heart is restless until it finds its rest in thee." What he was saying is that there was a hunger for being in the bosom of the cosmic God. But one thing our jaded contemporary culture has learned, and repeatedly forgets, is that whatever we desire when obtained is never enough! So, it has to be desired again, pursued again, and will disappoint again.

In the 1920s, Jung took a trip through America, and he traveled to the Taos Pueblo, where he had a lengthy interview with the leader of the Pueblo tribe. That leader said to Jung, and I paraphrase, "You Europeans [meaning the whole Anglo culture], you're such strange people. You're like the grasshoppers that come from time to time. You come, you devour, and you move on." He said, "What are you looking for? What is your hunger? Why would you be so hungry? We have it all here. All we have to do is look around and see the beauty of the world around us and the natural world that sustains us."

Gluttony is most problematic when it causes us to forget what really in the end feeds us best. Gluttony can be a kind of soporific or a surrogate for what is missing in us—a connection for what is really a treatment plan for loneliness or for connection.

One of the great pathologies of the human condition and, especially of our time of interconnectivity, is loneliness; and many turn to food as a constant object. I had a client who was abandoned as a child and grew up on the streets. He was severely obese because, as he said, the only constant in his life, and it was not constant very often, was food. Up to the time of therapy, he was unable to pass a fast-food place without indulging. So great was his fear of loss that he kept himself out of relationships as best as he could, which meant he was left with food as the sole other with which to connect. You can see the birth of addictions here is all about connecting with the other. Addictions are reflexive anxiety treatment plans.

That means the addictive connection—whether it is to food or a cigarette or a warm body or a substance or even power or money—temporarily lowers the level of internal discord. The key there is, of course, temporarily. It has to be repeated, and that's the addictive hook. Underneath the treatment of any addiction is the real haunting question: *Can I feel what I'm already feeling without the "treatment plan," a treatment plan that hooks me to other consequences?* Because if I can feel what I'm already feeling and already treating this in this inadequate way, then I find that this hunger no longer has such a tyrannous hold over my life. It reminds me of a client who was a long-term member of AA, who said, "We have a saying in our group: this isn't working for me, but I do it very well."

We all have our patterns of trying to meet our nurturant needs. Gluttony is taking that daily nurturant necessity and turning it into an end in itself. That's how, for example, sentiment becomes sentimentality. Sentiment—the capacity to have a feeling relationship to our world—is important. Sentimentality is being owned by an indulgence in that sentimentality, and ultimately gluttony distracts us from the question of what really feeds us. As the Greek poet Callimachus noted many, many centuries ago, "All that I have given to my stomach has disappeared, but I retain the fodder that I gave to my spirit."[2] In other words, the pleasure of the taste has disappeared, but I have the calories and other consequences of my habit.

If I were to use the word *epicurean*, you might think of fine dining. Ironically the pre-Socratic Greek philosopher Epicurus had no such intention. He properly noted millennia ago that human beings were pleasure-seeking, pain-avoiding creatures. That's not too hard to figure out, but he noted that there was a big disconnect between intensity and duration. He said, we go for intensity. But he was inquiring: What would provide duration for pleasure? What would nurture us? The question he was really asking was: What would sustain us? We know what distracts us, what excites us, but what would sustain us? Ironically, he would have thought eating was one of the greatest of intensities but least in duration. After it's past our taste buds, it becomes fodder for the lower regions. What he concluded—surprise, surprise, as a philosopher—was that the habit, the hunger, that was most sustaining was the hunger for truth, the hunger for knowing the mysteries; in short, philosophy best provided duration of satisfaction.

But each of us has to ask the question, *What is it that really feeds me?* In Dante's *Inferno*, Dante depicts how people seeking something on this planetary existence are given it in abundance in the future in order to see how well they really like that. The gluttonous, then, were condemned to eat rats, toads, snakes, and other good things as a kind of perverse reward. You want matter, you want connection, here it is, and how does that satisfy? So it might behoove us to ask the question, *What provides abiding satisfaction, sustained and sustaining pleasure?*

THE SIN OF LUST

Then we have our friend lust as a so-called sin. Remember that the ancients considered Eros a god. Eros was variously described as both the oldest of the gods, because at the beginning of all things, and the youngest, because renewing itself in every moment of being. It takes desire to begin something, so it's the archaic source of all things; and it is later capable of being evoked in any new moment of being. We can best translate Eros's desire as a desire for connection. The word *desire* comes from the Latin term *sidus*, translated "of the stars," meaning that which guides us. It was a term often used by mariners: if you can find the guiding star, you can plot your course; but lose the stars, and you are adrift and in trouble on the wine-dark sea.

Desire drives all things. We associate the absence of desire as synonymous with depression, even death. Desire historically has been associated with heat, with fire, consuming fire until spent. The Greek philosopher Heraclitus said all is fire and we are always burning. The essayist Walter Pater, in the nineteenth century, said, "To burn always with this hard, gemlike flame, to maintain this ecstasy, is success in life."[3] You may recall, from the twentieth century, the poet Edna St. Vincent Millay who said, "My candle burns at both ends. It will not last the night, but ah, my foes, and oh, my friends—it gives a lovely light."[4]

Desire is what starts the world every day. Where does it lead, then, is the question. And what is consummation of desire but to be consumed, annihilated? In Dante's *Inferno*, those who are caught in lust or compulsive desire are blown back and forth by strong winds. In other words, they are always at the mercy of the next strong wind, not possessors of their own souls.

We can always ask the question of any value or any pursuit: *What does this make me do? What does it keep me from doing?* And so it is. Lust is a normal human desire and only becomes pathological when it dominates. It's consumed only in the moment and fails to value what lasts, what sustains, what endures. As we know, its anarchic nature can be destructive to self, to committed relationships, to peace of mind. Even Augustine in his *Confessions* talks about his paradoxical prayer, "Oh, Lord, make me chaste. But not just yet, please. Not just yet."[5]

We also have to recognize the pathology of the repression of the natural. If we repress desire, what's going to happen to it? It will pathologize. It will show up in somatic illnesses, depression, self-medication, or acting out, as we have seen in so many accounts of people taking advantage of children or those within their power. We recognize that in that pathology and criminal activity is nonetheless the expression of the natural life force that was opposed, blocked in some way, and channeled in a way where the person couldn't celebrate the joy of natural erotic life.

We also have to ask: Why is it that we wish that annihilation through being consumed in the other? Well, remember life starts with profound and traumatic disconnection as the infant is expelled from the womb and thrust into an alien and threatening environment. Being conscious is also being mindful of one's separation from the other. Accordingly, the fundamental agenda of romance is to "die" in the other. In that moment, there is a healing of estrangement and a coming home through merging with the other. What the French called la petite mort, "the little death," orgasm, is a brief revisit to the cosmic absorption in the other. Rilke wrote a poem in which he talks about a couple making love and then ends the poem by saying, then "loneliness flows onward between them like the river."[6] Having merged, briefly, they return to the elemental human experience of isolation.

So lust is normal and natural even as its power threatens violence and harm to relatedness. Lust has been defined as desiring to sleep with someone, and love has been defined as wanting to wake up with them. There is a critical distinction. As with gluttony, one has to ask: *What abides, what sustains, what proves meaningful over time?* Can lust evolve into enduring love? We know what it is to be carried on the impulse of the moment. We also know where that can lead. It's part of our nature, and to deny that is pathologenic. At the same time, we're all accountable for asking, *How can I honor this elemental life force and sustain a lifelong relationship to desire, but at the same time, channel this most natural of energies into creative and committed forms of relationships?*

THE SIN OF ANGER

Anger or wrath is another one of the so-called deadly sins. It's always been interesting to me that the words *anger, anxiety, angst,* and *angina* come from the single Indo-Germanic root *angh*, which means "to constrict." When the organism is constricted, it will feel anxiety because its well-being is threatened. It will then feel secondarily anger to aggress against the aggressor. It will feel, of course, angst, which is the threat to its existential survival. Angina is the constriction of the heart. All represent constriction to the natural being and as such are registered by the psyche.

So if you were told as a child, as I was, that you are not to be angry, then you are in some way allied against your nature. It's a natural response to the perceived and actual abuse of the psyche and yet to be denied the natural response in return.

We often have what you might call a passive anger that then goes underground, shows up as avoidance, referred energies in an alternative direction, or passive-aggressive behavior. That's in contrast to active anger, which shows up in ordinary aggression between people up to and including road rage, warfare, and so forth.

Anger itself has served evolution by helping humans mobilize a defense through aggression toward that which threatened us. But we also know how destructive it can be. Many years ago, someone of another ideological persuasion said to one of my clients, "You should not waste time with the Jungians because they never talk about sex or aggression." All I could do was lamely protest. "Well, that's not true. We talk about sex and aggression. We're just not preoccupied with it." But what I really wanted to say was "Screw you." But that was not "proper." I never said that, but at least you and I know the difference. In analytic work, we have to deal with the anger that was so often repressed by the weight of adaptation required of the child. To bring this up and honor it without being driven by it is part of the healing that allows one to recover a relationship to the natural desires of the soul and not be walled off from them. But what happens when all that anger remains dammed up?

Anger denied goes somewhere, somaticizes, leaks out, or turns inward to become depression. Remember Ares, the god of anger, war—the Greek name; or the Latin version, Mars—was a god, and the gods must be served. When I was in Zurich, the book *Mars*, by a man whose pseudonym was Fritz Zorn, was published. *Zorn* is the German word for rage. It was a story of the young man in his late twenties who was dying from terminal cancer. He realized that his whole life had been constrained by the collective pressure to be consistent with the value system of his upper-class upbringing. He felt that his cancer was his body exploding in rage and repression.

Zorn got the idea that if he could write this book, essentially denouncing his family and Swiss respectability, that he might be able to get all that anger out of him and save his life. The book was published a day or two before he died of that cancer. It became a bestseller in Switzerland for understandable reasons. In it, you can see the book is his fist in the face of all of his conditioning. He comes to recognize that the greatest cost to his life was not his cancer. It was the repression of his natural feeling and spontaneous life. That was the great price that he had to pay, for which he had understandable anger. That anger accumulated through the years and became rage.

We also know that anger can play a powerful and destructive role in the world. That's hardly a recent revelation. *The Iliad* is often subtitled "The Wrath of Achilles." Achilles learned that his dear friend Patroclus was murdered by Hector after Hector saw Patroclus wearing the armor of Achilles and thought he had slain Achilles. Achilles picked up the broken body and the armor that his friend has been wearing. He lifted the broken armor between his hands, and we are told his eyes were like furnace doors ajar. Furnace doors ajar! Such is a timeless description of madness when one is possessed by the god Ares and incapable of responding in a measured way.

That's anger: furnace doors ajar. That anger pushes him across an invisible line, and when he ultimately triumphs over Hector, he degrades the body. He ties a throng around his Achilles tendon and drags Hector's body seven times around Troy while Hector's family watches. He is clearly possessed by Ares, by rage. He is driven berserk.

The word *berserk* originally came from wearing bear shirts. The Teutonic invaders often wore bear shirts as protection against the cold and against enemy arrows. They were known to rouse themselves into an animalistic blood rage. The clinical psychologist Jonathan Shay, in his book *Achilles in Vietnam*, wrote that the greatest pathology for soldiers is to have entered that state of unbalanced anger. His research indicated that those who went "berserk" were the most injured and suffered the largest number of continuing PTSD traumata.

So once again, what we see is that wrath or anger is a naturally occurring emotional response to the wounds and traumata and injustices of life and becomes pathological when it's unrestrained, when it's not balanced by its opposite. In fact, something that is unbalanced by its opposite becomes demonic, meaning that it's not checked by a compensatory emotion or compensatory value of some kind.

THE SIN OF PRIDE

Pride is another one of the sins, sometimes known as vanity or vanitas. What do we mean by the word *pride*? It's obviously changed somewhat in its meaning. Aren't we supposed to take pride in ourselves, our work, our family, our school? Pride is best translated by that old Greek word, which we still use, *hubris*. Pride as hubris might be translated as arrogance. Arrogance is arrogating to ourselves powers we don't properly deserve.

In modern psychological parlance, we call such hubris "inflation." Inflation means being in a state of self-delusion, forgetting the limits of our knowledge, believing that we know enough to be conscious, when we never know enough to know enough. Inflation means not knowing we don't know that we don't know. That's what's meant by the sin of pride. Such pride operates under the illusion of exemption—namely that I am exempt from the limitations and from the autonomous work of the gods.

As I pointed out earlier, what we call Greek tragedy was predicated on this assumption that our fatal flaw, our hamartia, was based on the presumption that we were exempt. Of course, what tragedy meant, dramatized on the stage, was that spiritual arrogance ultimately led people to make choices, and from those choices, consequences brought their downfall.

For Dante, in *La Commedia*, the prideful are humbled by being broken on the wheel. In a sense, ultimately, reality brings us all back to our common humanity. In medieval theology, pride surfaces a presumption that one can earn salvation rather than receive it as a gift of grace. We know it led to the excesses of the medieval church that caused the Reformation and many other schisms.

Another fine example of the temptation of pride is found in Homer's description of the battle between Hector and Patroclus—a scene that occurred before the one discussed above. Here is the astonishing account of what transpired when Hector meets Patroclus. Hector, thinking it's Achilles on the field of battle defeats his opponent. In the narrative, Patroclus was brought low not only by Hector's skills but by a youth who impaled his knees with a lance. And while Hector stands over his fallen opponent, Patroclus reminds him that it took three to kill him—a God, a boy, and last of all a hero. He tells Hector at his hour of greatest triumph that soon he, too, will be following into the underworld. Hector cannot help but pause and acknowledge the final democracy of death that awaits all, even heroes.

What we have in that marvelous piece of drama, from nearly three millennia ago, is the humbling that life inevitably brings to pride. Here is Hector, at the moment of his greatest hour, recalled to his humanity and to be reminded, at the moment of triumph: *And you are next in line, Hector.* The task of the artist is to call us to consciousness, especially consciousness regarding our limitations, and where those invisible lines are. If even Hector, Achilles, and that bright heroic assembly forget and cross the lines of restraint, how much more are we at risk?

THE SIN OF ENVY

Then we have our friend envy. You remember envy. H. L. Mencken once said that a puritan is a person who is desperately afraid someone somewhere is having a good time. Envy is predicated on the perception that someone else has what I want or need. Jealousy is something I have wedded to the fear that someone may take it away.

Sadly, jealousy has often been the chief source of domestic violence, where people feel threatened in the love and commitment of their partners and wind up, in grievous ways, succumbing to that insecurity. But envy is really based on the presumption that I'm not sufficient as I am—most of us think that, frankly—and therefore you or someone else are necessary to complete me.

Envy's a failure to remember that we're children of creation, whether that be a divine being or a natural process, and that we're all given what internal sources are actually needed inside. Contrary to pride, it's too easy for all of us to remember our limitations, to not trust, to not risk, to not believe in our great capacity, forgetting that we've been given all that we need to survive and to prevail on this journey we call our lives. Dante uses the metaphor of plunging the envious into freezing water, perhaps to lower the intensity of their yearning for what another possesses.

There is a wonderful correspondence between Rilke and a young man who wrote to him for advice at the beginning of the last century. Many of you have probably read Rilke's *Letters to a Young Poet*. Let me share a passage from that as Rilke's talking to the young man and his uncertainty. The young man has expressed his natural fears about life: Am I going to be sufficient? Can I cope with life? What do I need to know? This is what Rilke writes to him, and I think the words persist in their value to us:

We are set down in life as in the element to which we best correspond, and over and above of this, we have through thousands of years of accommodation become so like this life that when we hold still, we are scarcely to be distinguished from all that surrounds us. We have no reason to mistrust our world for it is not against us. Has it terrors? They are our terrors. Has it abysses? Those abysses belong to us. Are dangers at hand? We must try to love them. And if only we arrange our life according to the principle which counsels us, that we must always hold to the difficult. Then that, which seems to us most alien, will become what we most trust and find most faithful.

Then Rilke goes on to add to the young poet,

How should we be able to forget those ancient myths that are at the beginning of all peoples? The myths about dragons at the last moment turned into a princess. Perhaps all the dragons of our lives are princesses who are only waiting to see us once, beautiful and brave. Perhaps everything terrible in its deepest being is something helpless that wants help from us.[7]

Well, I think we all are touched by those moving words of Rilke, and we so easily forget them. Envy is also forgetful of the fact that we're all participants in the common democracy of fallibility, that we're all equals in the democracy of mortality.

One last example of this is also drawn from Western literature. Let's reflect on how Shakespeare's Richard II ironically notes how so many envied him in his royal state and how, having lost a critical battle, and now fallen, he speaks to his comrades.

Of comfort, no man speak:
Let's talk of graves, of worms and epitaphs;
Make dust our paper and with rainy eyes
Write sorrow on the bosom of the earth,
Let's choose executors and talk of wills:
And yet not so, for what can we bequeath
Save our deposed bodies to the ground?
Our lands, our lives and all are Bolingbroke's,
And nothing we call our own, but death

And that small model of the barren earth
Which serves as paste and cover to our bones.
For God's sake, let us sit upon the ground
And tell sad stories of the death of kings;
How some have been deposed; some slain in war,
Some haunted by the ghosts they have deposed;
Some poisoned by their wives: some sleeping killed;
All murdered. For within the hollow crown
That rounds the mortal temples of a king
Keeps death his court and there the antic sits,
Scoffing his states and grinning at his pomp,
Allowing him a breath, a little scene
To monarchize, be feared and killed with looks,
Infusing him with self and vain conceit,
As if this flesh which walls about our life,
Were brass impregnable, and humored thus
Comes at the last and with a little pin
Bores through the castle wall, and farewell king!
Cover your heads and mock not flesh and blood
With solemn reverence: throw away respect,
Tradition, form and ceremonious duty,
For you have mistook me all this while:
I live with bread like you, feel want,
Tasted grief, need friends: subjected thus,
How can you say to me, I am a king?[8]

Well, certainly Richard has joined the common democracy of all mortals and is very much like us. So much for envy.

THE SIN OF GREED

Then we have our old friend greed, also known as avarice. Again, greed is forgetting what truly sustains us. What feeds greed is more, ever more. Greed is a grand obsession of our time, a time when enough is never, never enough. Greed is especially prevalent among those who've lost their spiritual moorings, or lost direction in their journey, or forgotten that the journey is why they're here in the first place. In fact, it's fair to say that the great religion of the postmodern world is materialism—fill this emptiness, this spiritual emptiness, with matter of some kind. Thus, the great emptiness that we feel, the nibbling of existential angst at the periphery, is filled with objects upon which our impoverished souls have projected stability, continuity, ready availability, and even the faint hope of nurturance.

I had a client many years ago who had grown up in a time of great privation and, when he later came into wealth, he was compulsively driven to purchase multiple automobiles every year. He laughed at it as a strange obsession, which he could afford, but he was still a prisoner of it because when he was a child, a new automobile represented freedom, mobility, "away from here," and a larger life out there. His joke was when the window wiper fluid is empty, it's time to get a new car. He knew that it was driving him rather than the other way around, and yet so caught was he in the pathology of our time, of assuming the object itself is what is of value rather than what it represents to us, that he felt compelled to keep buying and buying.

In Dante's *Inferno*, the materialists, the greedy, those who spent their lives seeking matter were given it to the max. They were given boulders to push around through eternity. You want matter? You got matter—here it is.

Sometimes, as a therapist, I've asked people to put a garish sign on the door of their refrigerator or wherever else to confront some compulsive greed that they have, that says "That which I'm seeking I cannot find in here." I've often asked people to look at the obsession and ask, "What is it really about?" Greeds are never about what they're about, whether its food, money, power, sex. They're always ultimately about spiritual issues driven by fear, loneliness, emptiness, general anxieties, the absence of meaning.

It's wrong to judge those anxieties, for they are part of the human condition. But it's also pragmatic to ask if our greeds really produce effective treatment plans in the end. Remember my AA client who said, "This isn't working for me, but I do it very well."

A number of years ago, when I lived near Atlantic City, I was very much imbued with asking, "What is all of this gambling hoo-ha about?" The casinos in Atlantic City and Las Vegas were the most visited spots on the planet by pilgrims. By that, I mean, not people looking for their daily employment, not people who were driven there by wars and so forth, but people who were in search of something. For context, the annual hajj to Mecca is of 2.5 million people. The average attendance at Disney World and Disneyland is in a range of twelve to fifteen million per year.

At that time at least, the average attendance in pre-COVID-19 Las Vegas and Atlantic City was between thirty-three and thirty-six million apiece every year. Never in human history has there been a pilgrimage of that magnitude before, a massive movement of humans looking for something. So it's reasonable to ask,

"All right, what is it that brings people to the casinos?" The obvious answer is a good time, money, something like that, but there's something deeper than that going on, something invisibly driving those buses that pull in there at the rate of a thousand a day, filled with people often coming with the last of their savings.

I think what courses beneath the surface includes three things. First of all, they're looking for some kind of *connection*. Remember the word *religion* itself is a confession of disconnect. Etymologically it means "to reconnect, to bind back to." The religious motive in us is to reconnect with something that we feel separated from. The connection is the desire to link to that which is home or feeds us or somehow nurtures and sustains us.

Second, this mass enthusiasm is a search for that which lifts my life out of the ordinary, out of the pure horizontal definition of life, that our life is just the number of breaths we take before we stop breathing on this planet. None of us would be happy with that definition. We want something vertical in our lives. The fantasy is that money will somehow transform my life in a way that makes me better. For a moment, perhaps, I will transcend the ordinariness of this journey. So it's a search for *transcendence*.

The professional gambling industry also purveys the fantasy of *transformation*—that my life will be better off having connected, having more money, or having the oranges show up at the same time on the little spinning wheels or the dice showing up with the appropriate numbers, because each of those is an intuited connection with the invisible world, with the mystery that informs the material world.

I would submit to you that the search for connection, for transcendence, and for transformation are inherently religious needs, and as an increasing number of people are not finding them in contemporary religious institutions, they will be looking for them through the projected world gambling offers. As I said, when the numinous is not encountered, it will somaticize, it will show up as addictions, or we will be looking for it in the external world, through the objects upon which our projections fall. And what better example than the casinos to represent that.

Remember Augustine's words, "Our hearts are restless till they find their rest in Thee." For Augustine, these deep needs were found in his theological connection. As his answers have become convincing to fewer and fewer people, all the enticements of the secular religions of hedonism, materialism, and narcissism may be. Some of us can find rest for the restlessness in our souls, in a Thee, as Augustine did, and some cannot. For many of us, there's only a sense of disconnect, and greed for the thing out there offers to fill that empty space. So if we who are pilgrims cannot wind our way to Canterbury with Chaucer's pilgrims, there's always Atlantic City or Las Vegas.

THE SIN OF SLOTH

There's sloth too, another one of our deadly sins. I had planned to write about sloth at this point, but I'm tired now, and it's been a long day, so I think I'm going to take a nap for a while. Oh, okay, I'll finish. There is an enormous appeal of sleep, after all. Remember the two gremlins at the foot of our bed: fear and lethargy? Fear's intimidation is by whatever seems too large for us. Lethargy is the desire to sleep, to pull the blanket over our head and somehow wake to a different tomorrow. In Dante's *Inferno*, the slothful were placed in a pit of snakes. I guess that would quicken anyone's slumbering sensibilities. Remember what Jung said: we all desire to drown in the unconscious. On the other hand, the spirit of evil is negation of the life force by fear. Only boldness can deliver us from our fears, and if the risk is not taken, the meaning of life is violated.

As we've seen, we have so many ways of avoiding, succumbing to sloth, resting easy in the saddle, simple avoidance, forgetfulness, suppression, denial, repression, disassociation, and projection onto others. Maybe the subtlest is the search for magic. We can even find intellectual and spiritual sloth in pop psychologies and feel-good theologies. It is subtle, but so often we're looking for magic to help us finesse the difficulties of life. That reminds me of a recent visit to a bookstore, where I asked the salesperson, "Can you show me to the self-help section?" She said, "Yes, I could, but doing so would be self-defeating, wouldn't it?"

SEVEN STATES OF PSYCHOLOGICAL POSSESSION

What is the hero or the heroine? Jung defined it as a specific cluster of energy in the psyche that is given to us by nature. It's tasked with overthrowing the darkness, the darkness of fear, the darkness of sloth.

On the printer in my office, I have a brief quote from Odysseus: "I will stay with it and endure through suffering hardships; but once the heaving sea has shaken my raft to pieces, then, I will swim."[9] Well, why should Odysseus swim? Does it all not end in death? Is not so much of life fringed with defeat, decay, desuetude, depression, and despair? That's the voice of the tempter that tells us that life is too hard, the struggle's not worth it; that there's nothing still to discover about ourselves, about one another, about the world, about the great mystery of being; and that this discovery may continue through the last breath of our lives.

At the same time, as we know, when we think about the concept of sin, too great a sense of sinfulness is a terrible burden, a weight that colors and oppresses every day, which is why our cultures evolve confession, collective scapegoating, and renewal, like Ash Wednesday, Yom Kippur, and so on. But the concept of sin also explains why forgiveness and grace are necessary. I've always appreciated the Christian philosopher and theologian Paul Johannes Tillich's definition of grace where he implored that we accept the fact that we are accepted despite the fact of being unacceptable.

The world has been full of utopian visions and perfect societies, and all have fallen apart. All fell apart because of human nature prevailing in its many perverse forms. As far back as Plato, we were told we do not do evil deliberately: we do evil out of ignorance, hence the importance of reason and education. And I buy that, in part, but it's also called the "Socratic fallacy."

In the nineteenth century, Dostoevsky, in his *Notes from Underground*, critiques that, speaking of the Socratic fallacy, we don't do wrong deliberately. He says,

> Oh, tell me, who was it who first announced, who was it first proclaimed that man only does nasty things because he does not know his interests; and if he were enlightened, if his eyes were open to his real normal interests, man would at once cease to do nasty things, would at once become good and noble because, being enlightened and understanding his real advantage, he would see his own advantage in the good and nothing else, and we all know that not one man can, consciously, act against his own interest, consequently, to say, through the necessity, he would begin doing good? Oh, the babe! Oh, the pure innocent child![10]

In other words, so much of history, as Dostoevsky points out, is a refutation, that there are times we just deliberately pull the roof down on our heads, even exult in our capacity for destruction. That's why the theologian Reinhold Niebuhr so famously said, our capacity for justice makes democracy possible, but our proclivity to injustice also makes it necessary.

When we reflect on these seven deadly sins, or states of psychological possession, or visitations, we have to come to the fact that underneath four of these sins is an unconscious conclusion: I'm not enough in myself. I must solicit and possess some other. Those are greed, lust, envy, and gluttony.

In the last chapter, you might have asked, How do I manage the shadow? Well, as you know, we don't manage the shadow; we just try to avoid its managing us all the time. It's the same with sin. We don't avoid sin; it's intrinsic to our humanity, a constant presence in our daily lives. But it's been said that all the gods ask of us is not perfection—that's reserved for them—but humility and the remembrance of them. This is why Jung said, quite tellingly, the greater the light, the longer the shadow. Remember his notion: our task is not goodness, for goodness would only prove one-sided and bring forth unexpected darkness sooner or later. Our task is wholeness, a fuller expression of our human possibilities.

There's a report in the Gnostic Gospel of Thomas in the words of Jesus, where Jesus meets a person who's laboring on the Sabbath, which was sinful in that culture. He said, if you know what you're doing, you are saved. If you don't know what you're doing, you are damned. I think what that Gnostic indication was is this: If you have a compelling reason for breaking the law, and this has been carefully sorted through, then you are not bound by the law. But if you're simply doing that impulsively and out of your own sense of inflated righteousness, then you have a problem. Maybe that's what Augustine meant when he said, "Sin consciously."

Part of our task, then, is to remember these so-called sins, to observe them rise in familiar ways every day, and to begin to discern their patterns in the unfamiliar. For they're never far from us, nor are we far from them. Avoid them? We can't. We remain, in Nietzsche's phrase, human, all too human. Let's also remember, as good old Samuel Beckett, the novelist and playwright, put it: "Failed? Fail again. Fail better." Or maybe better is simply as Augustine suggested, if we're going to sin, sin consciously at least.

5

Dispelling the Ghosts Who
Run Our Lives

W e all live in haunted houses and sleep in memory's unmade bed. In this chapter, we're going to look at the presence of the past that's with us all the time—what I call "hauntings."

THE HUMAN PSYCHE IS TIMELESS

While housed in a fragile frame, the human psyche is timeless. That's how you can suddenly dream of a child you knew in third grade and perhaps haven't seen in decades, remember an old schoolteacher, or revisit some moment in your history that was long ago and far away. In those moments, you realize the timelessness of the psyche. Everything that's ever happened is present, recorded, and often "storied," as you've read in prior chapters. What are the stories that we evolved, consciously or unconsciously, around those moments?

Photographs are examples of how we consciously seek to retain a link to our past. Why do we take photos? We're trying to freeze the moment. We're trying to stay the passage of time and be able to go back to it and somehow recreate it. In that little frame, we have a whole welter of emotions and untold stories. But all that has happened is stored intrapsychically in any case. It not only remains there, waiting to be activated, but it carries a quantum of energy capable of moving us to tears, unwitting behaviors, and occasionally moments of insight.

Diane Wakoski wrote a fascinating poem titled "The Photos."[1] She recounts a rather painful visit with her mother and sister. It's clear there is much unspoken, much history, and many ghosts. She constantly refers to her "well-dressed" sister and her more casual self as well as her mother's sour and critical presence.

On the table is a photograph of her father, the former husband of her mother. She makes a passing reference to it, and suddenly everything comes down to that photo, which stirs up all the memories of the past. It becomes very uncomfortable for all. She has to get out of there, so she makes an excuse and drives off toward her home. As she's driving down the highway, all she can do is think about her mother's face and how she inherited that face. She sees her reflection in the rearview mirror as she crosses lanes, she sees her mother's face staring back at her, and she realizes she is still haunted, owned by that history, which she has been so desperate to escape.

Clearly the photo contains a lot of history and a lot of "ghosts." Given that she's a poet, I'm sure she pays careful attention to what each word means. She could have said, "Oh, I don't like the fate that brought me into this particular marriage, this particular family, this particular history." But instead she says "destiny," almost implying as much as she tries to flee, as much as she wishes to get away, history pursues her. History's haunting is even imprinted in the face that she's inherited from the mother from whom she is so estranged.

In prior chapters we looked at the distinction between fate and destiny. We ask ourselves, why is life so difficult? Is it because others are out to get us? Is it others who are making us miserable from time to time? Is it the forces of fate or malevolent gods? Are we ourselves inadequate? What is it that creates so many difficulties in our lives? What is the source of the interferences, the strange places from which our choices come and the patterns evolve?

You might remember that one of the ways to begin to dialogue with the unconscious—which by definition almost seems impossible because the unconscious is unconscious—is the recognition of patterns in our lives, especially those we find troubling, problematic, perhaps hurtful to ourselves and to others. We realize that those patterns arise out of "presences," whether conscious or often not conscious, and that our behavior is in service, in a sense, to the instructions of those assumptions, those premises. Where do they come from? How do we get them?

We are creatures who "story" our lives in an effort to make sense of them. We need and grow attached to our narratives, even if they're inaccurate. The task of depth psychology is really to try to track the invisible world that moves through the forms of the visible world. We can't know about the unconscious by definition; rather, only as it manifests in the work of daily life can we begin to see traces of it. We have to work backward from that which is tangible into the realm of the invisible. Then we begin to realize that all of us are in service to what I might loosely and metaphorically call "spectral presences."

POSSESSION AND SOUL LOSS

The human condition has not changed. Our ancestors were aware of these spectral presences. They didn't apply the lens of depth psychology perhaps, but they talked about those spectral presences of the past. Sometimes they called them ghosts, evil spirits, zombies, curses. In 1919, Jung wrote the very interesting essay, "The Psychological Foundations of Belief in Spirits." In that essay, he describes how the belief in the invisible presences, the hauntings of ethereal beings, is found in all cultures, past and present.

This notion of the presence of the invisible is a universal experience, and how do we account for that? Are we to assume that there are in fact ghosts and visitations of people from the otherworld? He goes on in the essay to make a very critical and telling remark: "Spirits, when viewed from the psychological angle, are unconscious autonomous complexes, which appear as projections because they have no direct association with the ego."[2]

That's a very rich and pregnant sentence. Notice how when he writes, "Spirits, when viewed from a psychological angle," he's not ruling on whether there are presences from an occult origin. "When viewed from a psychological angle, are unconscious . . ." indicates I'm not aware of their presence, and "autonomous complexes" means they have a life of their own. "Complexes" refers to charged clusters of energy, which appear to us through projections. Remember, projections are not something we do consciously. When the psyche is triggered by either an inner event or outer stimulus, a projection can result. Certain energies leave me and go out into the world "because they have no direct association with the ego." In other words, I don't realize this mechanism is at work.

That sentence is helpful because it reminds us to realize how often we're not dealing with the world as it is but as our projections onto it allow us to see it. Now again, a projection is one of the psyche's ways of trying to make the new moment (and every moment is new) familiar. Where have I been here before? What do I know about this? What helps me explain this or relate to this in a productive way? Of course, because of that, we often unwittingly falsify the absolute uniqueness of the other at that moment. We can't help doing that, but because it has no direct association with the ego, we don't know that we've done that. Recall, as the philosopher Immanuel Kant observed, if one wears blue spectacles, one can only see blue forms in a blue world.

As I mentioned earlier, along with projection comes transference: What has been my history of behavior, the script of expectations? What is this mechanism that leads to the repetitions, the patterns that we've been describing? It's a very interesting way of reflecting on how little we actually know what it is we're seeing and from whence it comes.

Part of the task of depth psychology is less to explore that outer phenomenon as it is to see from whence it comes within us and what internal engines produce that phenomenon and give it such a compelling nature. Think about when one falls in love, perhaps with a total stranger. What one has surrendered to is one's own intrapsychic imago of the other, bearing little or no relationship to the outer figure. The same can also be true of reactions of fear. That's what paranoia is: transferring the trauma of a particular situation or experience to the new moment and unwittingly prejudicing that new moment.

Our ancestors certainly recognized that there are times when our psyche can be in states of possession. When Jung talked about how a complex is triggered, he described it as "ergriffenheit." It's the condition of being seized or possessed. In other words, our ego state is temporarily possessed by a psychic presence.

One of the few moments we're conscious during a daily activity is perhaps when we step into a shower. If the water's too hot or too cold, we make an adjustment. That's the ego standing in correct relationship to the world as it is at that moment. But from that moment on, we are often flooded with other material whether we're aware of it or not. Some of it we're aware of, like getting to work on time or taking care of the children or something of that sort. But many times we're not aware of the presence of that psychological energy, that spectral presence, and of course, we're seeing the world through whatever lens it allows us to employ.

Reflecting on the commonality of the human condition, our ancestors often described that state of possession as a loss of soul. There's an old Egyptian text from three millennia ago titled *The World-Weary Man in Search of His Ba. Ba* was the word for soul, and the notion that one could be separated from one's soul, or one's soul could have an experience of possession, is millennia-old.

Shamanic healing traditions were also based on the premise that some noxious spirit had stolen a piece of the soul. The shaman's task was to enter the psychic space of that person through a trance state to try to discern what was going on in the inner world of that person, to identify what spirit had been offended or neglected and was exacting revenge, to go deal with it, to fight with it if need be, or to conciliate it. The shaman did whatever it took, maybe through a compensatory set of behaviors that had a healing effect, to help restore that piece of the soul to the psyche of the suffering individual.

We have to remember what is not conscious may often still be present. Of course, what is present but not conscious is especially powerfully influential in our lives. As we know, the past may be forgotten but it is never wholly past.

CULTURAL COMPLEXES

We not only have a psychological history, and Diane Wakoski's poem "The Photos" was an account of one troubled family. The triggering event, the catalytic moment, was experiencing the photo revivify that history. For once they're united as a family— the missing father, the two hostile sisters, the angry and bitter mother—they're all present in the moment, and history is palpable and moving among them. In addition to the personal history, we also have a cultural history that all of us live in at all times. There are cultural possessions, cultural complexes.

A number of years ago, my wife and I were traveling in Germany and Poland, and we stayed for a while in Krakow. While there, we walked through the former Jewish ghetto in the Kazimierz district. In the central square was a series of very large chairs. There must have been thirty of them—all metal, all empty. It was commemoration of the presence of all of those absent. It was here that people were assembled often at gunpoint and put on the train for a roughly one-hour trip to the little village of Oswiecim, better known to us as Auschwitz. One sees in that ghetto, those empty chairs, not only Oskar Schindler's nearby factory that was made famous later but also the psychological horror and the presence of a great crime that is still in some way palpably there.

The Polish poet Adam Zagajewski has given us a warning about that as he slipped along those haunted streets in Krakow. He writes of walking the paths of Kazimierz and thinking of those not there, and yet "the eyes of the missing are like water and can't be seen—you can drown in them."[3]

And so it is, for that line suggests again the palpable presence of the past. There are cultural complexes that we're all born into. We all have to deal with received forms of behavior expectations. For example, for good or ill, gender roles and expectations are part of the psychological heritage that we've all received. Our ancestors, our parents, and our grandparents in most cases believed that these definitions were derived directly from God or from nature itself. Because the following decades spent a lot of time and effort deconstructing them, today we realize that they are in fact human constructs and not in the ontological nature of nature, even as their psychic influence upon people has been telling.

The playwright Henrik Ibsen noted this in his famous play *Ghosts*, which was a kind of fist in the face of societal ossification back in Oslo in 1882. One of the characters says,

> I'm inclined to think that we're all ghosts . . . It's not only the things
> that we've inherited from our fathers and mothers that live on in us,
> but all sorts of old dead ideas, and old dead beliefs, and things of that

sort. They're not actually alive in us, but they're rooted there all the same, and we can't rid ourselves of them. I've only to pick up a newspaper, and when I read it, I seem to see ghosts gliding between the lines. I should think there must be ghosts all over the country, as countless as grains of sand, and we were all, all of us so pitifully afraid of the light.[4]

What Ibsen saw in Norway at that time is certainly true of every culture. Each has received forms of experience, cultural patterns, admonitions, and behavior expectations, all of which have powerful influence upon people's choices. People usually violate them at great cost.

We only begin to make these invisible presences evident when we're obliged to, often by consequences piling up, reflect on what's happening in our lives. For example, as I've suggested, look at your patterns: From whence do they come? Or sometimes think about the strange mood states we find ourselves in. We might find ourselves with things going well at work, or at home, or whatever, but we remain caught in a peculiar mood—a mood of disquietude, a mood of somber reflection, or a mood of vague longing. Where is that coming from?

Somehow, such invisible players in the conduct of our lives bespeak other psychological realities that we all carry, even if unaware by the ego at that point. Of course, dreams in some way, too, are psychic possessions. I remember as a child thinking that a dream was somehow an actual event or a journey that had been taken, and many ancient traditions thought that as well. These are states of ego possession in which we are visiting a wholly different realm of our being, a mythopoeic realm that exists in all of us. People can, from an ego standpoint, dismiss all of their dreams as gibberish, nonsense, or just processing daily life. Yet sleep researchers have discovered that if we live to eighty, six years of our lives will be spent dreaming. Nature must have some purposeful intent in such a commitment of energy.

There's an old German phrase, "dreams are froth" (traume sind schaeme), meaningless, nothing. But in fact, if we pay attention, we realize these dreams are pointing toward profound psychological states of being—perhaps neglected issues that are asking our attention or are offering a corrective perspective on how our life is going from its vantage point.

I knew a woman who had lost a child and refused to mourn. She kept herself buried into busyness for some time. As events construed later, she was visiting a place that triggered the memories, and she saw that child coming toward her as an outer event. What had been pushed underground so deeply in some way then had to express itself. It had a quantum of energy that was not to be denied.

As we know, projections are unconscious, but what intent do they have, what issues are they bringing to the fore? When we see something like a projection, we naturally think it's real because it has all of the compelling qualities of reality. But for the woman who lost her child, it allowed the genuine beginning of necessary mourning and grieving.

THE CONCEPT OF THE COMPLEX

We have to remember the presence of those large figures in our lives we call the "parent complexes." Too often people think we're just blaming parents. That's not the point at all. It's rather to ask the question, in how many ways are the parents' presences still here, even when they are deceased? Perhaps they express themselves supportively, perhaps in an admonishing way, perhaps in a hurtful way. It's not a question of whether they're there; it's how they are there, what their messages are, and what influence plays out through our choices.

In traditional cultures, the presence of the parental complex was so strong as to be an object of reverence or sometimes fear. Spontaneous memories of parents, for example, were often interpreted as actual visitations by the deceased.

Thus, when the memory image of his dead parent suddenly appears to one of the ancients, it is as if it were her ghost that he sees and hears. Given the historic strengthening of the ego orientation of modernism, we are more likely to name these moments "flashbacks" or "memories," but in earlier times, charged imagoes were frequently considered occult visitations worthy of fear or reverence or both.

We may feel superior to our predecessors, but we are equally gullible when falling in love or having fear-based reactions to strangers. In those moments, we are just as possessed by our intrapsychic contents as visited our ancestors.

We are in some way caught up in our own psychological material, and yet we don't know that, so we respond to it as if it comes to us from the outer world. As we've also discussed, we have symptoms that serve as correctives or summons to consciousness. As a result, we often have to stop and pay attention and ask: *What's going on in here? Where does this come from? Why, when I am trying to do the right thing, make good choices, do these interferences with my plans interrupt and redirect me?*

I began the book with questions: Why is life so difficult? Why do things keep going wrong or getting messed up? We come back to familiar places, even though the outer context is overtly changed. I've always been haunted, and I think in a constructive way, by Jung's comment that what we do not make conscious will find a way to enter our lives nonetheless.

That's actually a very inviting but also scary thought. That of which I am unconscious will tend to come to me as fate. In other words, what I don't know about—say, the presence of my primal stories; of reflexes regarding trust, distrust, approach, avoidance, my parental material, other cultural influences, or other clusters of my history—will show up constantly in my relationships with my partner or my children or my neighbors. I think I am responding strictly to the exigencies of the present, but the invisible hand once again plays a role in the topography of our history. So, it's fair to say, complexes are "hauntings." In fact, maybe you found me out by now by realizing that I'm really talking about complexes here and employing the metaphor of hauntings because we've all heard the word *complex* and perhaps think of it simply as a pathological invasion. But complex theory is based on the notion that the past is never wholly past but may play a palpable role in the formation of our journey.

Jung didn't create the concept. It was created by a Berlin psychiatrist in 1895, but Jung recognized in the first decade of the last century how complex theory could describe something psychodynamic and formative in all of us. Of all of Jung's concepts, I suppose the one that is most practical, and the one I think about virtually every hour, is the idea of the complex.

A complex occurs because we have history. If I'm told as an infant or as a toddler, "Don't touch the oven or that hot pot. You're going to get hurt." I may or may not pay attention to that, but sooner or later I touch it. I now have an experience with a message. From that moment, there's always going to be a little cluster of history informing me. "Don't touch a pot on a stove" is protective.

Similarly, when I start to cross the street without thinking about it, I tend to look left and right, which is a protective complex. That's where the past can be instructive to us, and we can build upon it. But there are also times in which it infiltrates the present and contaminates it with the data of the past. First, think of a complex as a cluster of energy that's risen out of our experience and charged with a certain amount of energy. When it is triggered, it occupies our body. One of the ways to begin to recognize the complex at work is that we have familiar places where it'll show up in our body. Think of how your body registers anxiety before an emotional challenge. For one person, the complex will somaticize as a flutter in the stomach; for someone else, perhaps trembling extremities, or a constriction of the throat, or tightness in the chest, or whatever. It always occupies the body in some felt way.

Second, complexes always provide an addendum of energy to a situation. One of the ways to recognize the presence of a complex in ourselves or someone else is that the amount of energy being experienced or expended is in excess of the requirement of the situation. Unfortunately, often when we're in the grips of it, we think whatever we're saying or feeling is wholly appropriate to the situation. But later you might stop and reflect, *Why did I get so upset yesterday? Or why did I comply and give away my integrity one more time?*

Then one realizes, *I was in a possessed state. I was in a complex at that point.* Every complex, then, has a lens through which we see the world. It is a lens ground by history. That's why Wakoski's poem "The Photos" is in a sense saying, the photo itself brought all of us back to a moment where we saw who we were and who one another was through the murky lens of that troubled history. Is that fair? Not necessarily. But it's certainly part of the real history. It's also true that each of those clusters of energy contains a story, a partial story. It may be fragmentary, like don't touch a hot object. It may be very elaborate, such as we saw in Wakoski's poem—a whole family history of continuing estrangement.

Complexes occur because history occurs, and it's not pathological to have complexes. It's pathological to think we don't have them, or that we're not in them for a good part of every day. The man who purchased multiple cars every year, whom I mentioned in the prior chapter, illustrates an example of how complexes play out as psychic possessions. Remember, he had grown up in a very harsh, economically pressed family setting. For the child, the shiny object driving down the street was a numinous summons to a better world, a larger world. It was freedom, mobility, and "away from here."

As an adult, and having acquired affluence, he spent a lot of money on these cars over and over and over, and always with a diminishing sense of satisfaction or payoff. (There's certainly a sort of gluttony there, one of the deadly sins.) If one is not enough: *I have to have more.* Of course, part of the problem here is he was understandably confused about the distinction between a symbol and a sign. In other words, for the child, the car was a symbol. It pointed to the inexplicable, the world out there to which I want to escape. But a sign is a specific reference to an object or content. The symbol points beyond itself to that which one otherwise can't describe but can experience intuitively. The sign is the object upon which it falls. So purchasing automobile after automobile after automobile would be the equivalent of thinking, *Okay, now that I own the car, I have now that psychological freedom. I have that mobility.* Which in fact he had, yet he remained an unwitting prisoner of that psychological nexus of influences in the family. The literal could not touch the symbolic as so many find in a culture of materialistic hungers.

We can realize how his life, as many of our lives are, was governed by a kind of core complex. He felt defined by an emotional impoverishment that his affluence could never successfully treat. Many times, people spend much of their adult life compensating for feelings of inadequacy and, even more, surrendering to those feelings of inadequacy and being self-defeating every day. When they do that, they're caught in the past; they're psychologically possessed.

Here's another example of how complexes play out as psychic possessions. Remember the story of one of the great financiers, one of the 1990s arbitragers who wound up in the long run going to jail for manipulating the markets, even though he had, at one point, a personal fortune of over $400 million. (Far more than you and I made all last month.) He said his philosophy of life was "the person at the end of life who dies with the biggest pile is the one who wins." I remember thinking, *For a very smart person, what a sad and infantile philosophy of life that is. The biggest pile of what? Pile of sand? Pile of dirt? Pile of money? And, oh, yeah, and you're dead, remember?* So, there's an example of a person being psychologically possessed. I don't know his history, but I could imagine that there was one time when he profoundly felt the inadequacy of the world around him, the deficit out of which he was trying to operate and spent his life acquiring those dazzling numbers, those bank accounts that might seemingly treat the sense of emptiness.

Another specific example from history is Henry Kissinger, who was born in Fürth, a suburb of Nuremberg. He experienced the rise of antisemitism and the Nazi horror and was able to escape with his family. Someone later wrote about Kissinger, "Could you imagine that someone as powerful as Kissinger would not have been afraid of the Hitler *Jugend*, or the Hitler youth?" And I thought, *No, that's exactly the problem.* As a child, he would've naturally been terrified by those youthful thugs, and we see how he was driven through overcompensation to positions of power all of his life. He rose to being not only an advisor to the president but also a mover and shaker in world affairs. This is a person who said, "Power is the only aphrodisiac." Well, that's a person still in a complex; that's a person still possessed.

THE UNFINISHED BUSINESS OF THE PARENT

Psychic possessions can be so systemic that they literally create the pattern of a person's life. Think of the constrictive effects of bigotry, gender roles, ethnic constrictions. Because those pathogenic devices frame our sense of reality, and because such "stories" are so systemic, so compelling, so repetitive, and so requisite for approval among one's kind, we become all the more prisoner of a received definition. We don't really step out of such frames and question their legitimacy until something radical happens. This is why the intrapsychic imago of parents is so profound. On a conscious level, yes, they serve as models, some of which is overt and conscious, and some of which is not. But from them we also get an elemental sense of permission or lack of permission. Are you really free to have this life independent from their wishes? Are you able to live your journey, desire what you desire, seek what you seek, or do you have to somehow meet the conditions, justify your choices?

One of the biggest projects of the second half of life is to recover a sense of permission. Most people do not feel permission to live their journey. It's because we learned early that life is conditional, and you better learn to meet the conditions if you want love, approval, and support. We also learn blockages— where the parents are stuck, we'll tend to be stuck or we'll have to spend a lot of time trying to get unstuck, which is what leads to overcompensation. There's also the psychological effect of the unfinished business of the parent. Where did the parents steer around important issues, fail to address them in their life, and therefore show us, in some way, a model of stuckness or avoidance? This is not to blame the parent, for the parent is someone else's child who's struggling with their own psychological history.

This notion of the ancestral blockage is very important as well, just as we have long religious and cultural traditions that tend to permit one kind of behavior and block the others. But they, too, are psychic possessions. You'll recognize this in Jung's memoir, *Memories, Dreams, Reflections*. He looked at his own life and concluded that he had inherited the unfinished business of his ancestors. Their reluctance to move beyond the dogma-bound past to address questions posed by the modern spirit fell to him to address. So it is in many families that unaddressed matters roll over and flood the agenda of the children.

Jung came from a family of six clergy, including his father, which is quite a load. He always felt that they were deeply mired in dogma and in the expectations of the institution but had very little sense of a living faith, nor did they wrestle with what he considered the dark side of Divinity. He experienced his father's chronic depression, his sense of learned helplessness, the by-product of this grand avoidance. He felt that all oppression rose from his father's failure to find the courage to ask honest questions about what he believed and why he believed, and the failure to do so affected his emotional state throughout his life. Jung realized that legacy was part of the unfinished business that his family had presented to him to sort through: What is our proper relationship to the life of the spirit in the modern age, outside the field of institutional definitions? That became Jung's defining life question.

The parents are often the chief generators of our primal complexes, for they are omnipresent or notably absent in the child's formative hours. Each of us, as children, had to confront such questions as: Is the world safe or not? Can I believe what I believe and pursue what I want to pursue, or do I have to meet the conditions? Am I okay in myself, or do I have to twist and torque myself into something acceptable to the other person? Those kinds of psychic influences play out through our entire lives until such time as we make them conscious and take them on.

Let me give you a very moving example of this playing out in history. This is the story of my work with a man I'll call Jeffrey. He was an older man by the time I saw him in therapy, and his wife had passed away. His married life had been a long and fruitless struggle to save a severely alcoholic wife. He had adult children, including a functional competent daughter living in another city, whom he was going to visit. On the surface, a perfectly normal thing to do—a parent visiting a child. But because she had some relational difficulties in her life at that point, he was going on a rescue mission. You could say, "What's wrong with that?" Well, not necessarily anything except maybe that in reality perhaps the daughter doesn't need to be rescued. Maybe she can take care of things herself. But even more importantly, maybe he's also in service to an old complex because in his life history, his father had been a traveling salesman who was very honest and hardworking but gone almost all the time. So Jeffrey, as the eldest child, got enlisted as his mother's companion.

Early on, he got a de facto message: You are here to take care of this troubled woman. You are here to make her life better. That was the unfinished business of the relationship between two adults, but because it was not sufficiently addressed by them, guess what—the project falls upon the child. Jeffery picks this up and gets a lifelong message. On some deep level, that was probably a factor in his choosing a particular woman with drinking issues to marry to recreate his old role as the comforter of the wounded woman.

So here he is now, the third generation, dealing with the self-imposed rescue mission, and he had a dream the night before he departed to visit her in which his psyche makes all of this abundantly clear *and* critiques the complex. The Self, which is the place from which our dreams come, as Jung pointed out, certainly is a larger reality than the splinter personality of the complex. The complex and the Self are in contention with each other in this dream. This is such a profound and dramatic dream that speaks for itself.

"My mother has died. She's in a black casket in front of me. My father and others are there, but they are shadows and say nothing and glide away out of sight. A doctor and I are going to do an autopsy on the body in the casket." And by the way, he associated the doctor's presence as his therapist. So they're going to do an autopsy on this history.

"But I don't want to do it. The doctor says we must do it, so someone gets the benefit from it. I assume someone will get the information from this autopsy. I think, though, *Why me? Is this too much for a husband, but okay for a son?*"

See there again, there's something in his psyche saying, *You're carrying here the business of the father in the relationship with his wife, your mother, but it's still a job fallen to you.*

"The doctor looks like an old-time magician dressed all in black. He has a long rod with which to pry open the casket. I'm afraid of getting a disease from the decayed body. The doctor opens the casket; a woman in a long black dress with puffed shoulders is lying there. She does not look like my mother at any time in my mother's life. This woman looks young, thirty-something, and does not look dead. Now I see that it's Janine." Janine is his deceased wife. So the mother morphs into his deceased wife.

"She moves as though awakening from sleep before the doctor can touch her. She pushes herself up with her hands so that her upper body is against the lid and is facing us. I'm thinking it's Janine, and I don't want her back alive. The doctor says, 'They would be better off to leave them alone.' I assume he means the woman in the casket and people like her. He moves to kill her with the rod and close the casket. I yell, 'No!' and stop him. I'm horrified at the body coming back to life, but I'm even more horrified at killing her now again. The woman berates the doctor, scolds him, and calls him by condescending names, like she knows him well. I'm frozen, huddled up, waiting. She gets out of the casket. She walks away. She says, 'I rule here, I'm back.' Now she floats swiftly through the air toward me. She kisses me on the lips and quickly floats away like a dark shadow and disappears. The taste of her kiss on my lips is acid bitter."

Well, what a dream that is! Who would make that up? Notice here how this dream allows him to acknowledge the ambivalence today that he couldn't really acknowledge back then. He doesn't want that experience again, he doesn't want that assignment again; and the repetition of that assignment is in effect for him the kiss of death. But again, remember the context in which this dream occurs. He's about to leave the next morning on a goodwill mission to "rescue a third-generation of troubled women." This is not by the request or expectation of his daughter; it's the ancestral assignment that he has served.

I always found that such a profound and moving dream is salutary because it allowed him to really begin to examine the question: When is a good thing not a good thing? On the surface, a parent helping out an adult child is a good thing, but when it's in service to an archaic ancestral assignment, maybe it's not necessarily a good thing.

OUR RELATIONAL GHOSTS

We all have relational ghosts. Their programming of primal relationships invariably shows up in our subsequent relationships, in our friendships and associations, but most of all in our intimate relationships because the field of intimate relationship is ubiquitous, makes more demands upon us, and is there every day to reinforce the dynamic. In such relationships, we are less in our persona world, first of all; and second, they activate the primal paradigm of self and other forged in the smithy of childhood experience. They hit far deeper material than, say, our work relationships are likely to trigger. This is why marriages so often replicate the dynamics of one's earliest history.

We talked in a previous chapter about the patterns of existential adaptation to the threats of overwhelment and abandonment. Take the mother who inadvertently promoted her son to be her emotional companion because her husband was traveling so much, for example. Imposing such expectations was an invasion of the child's boundaries and the child's capacities. So that becomes the defining frame of how the child relates to people thereafter.

When people have had the experience of invasion or incursion into their psychic space—and we all have to some degree—they develop patterns of avoidance. You have to stop and ask yourself: *Where is it that I shy away from dealing with conflictual things in life? Where do I avoid dealing with what I know I need to deal with? Where do I find myself postponing or rationalizing?*

Well, we can work backward and say, *All right, that's a spectral presence in my life. That is the presence of that old, old story. That's a haunting.* We can inquire: *Where do I get caught in power complexes, where do I wind up trying to control the other person to bend them to my will? Or failing to do that, when do I engage in passive-aggressive behavior?* Passive-aggressive behavior is the power game of those who don't feel they have power, so one exercises power through subterfuge. Often we might wind up in patterns of compliance where we repeatedly sacrifice our legitimate needs; reflexively push aside our own will, desire, and legitimate expectations in life. Maybe we grow angry at our partner, or later the next day, reflect on why we did that, little recognizing at the time we were in the grip of a psychic possession.

Then there are those who experienced the opposite in childhood: the insufficiency of the primal other. That's often interpreted by a child through what's called "magical thinking"—namely, I am my experience rather than life is just stuff happening. The experience of insufficiency often leads to diminished self-worth with avoidant patterns and self-sabotage. We avoid fighting for the kind of life we want because inwardly we feel unworthy, inadequate, or insufficient. Or we get caught in a compensatory grandiosity: *Look how rich I am or how powerful I am, or look at my intelligent children*—all of which are compensation for inner feelings of inadequacy.

Maybe we get caught in the problem of power—the narcissistic need to control others and manipulate them one way or the other to make them serve our shaky sense of importance or value. Or we can get caught in compulsive neediness: constantly needing reassurance, constantly looking to the other, constantly testing their affection, and so forth. Because of that, we wind up pushing them away from us naturally and then wonder why they've done that to us once again. We have that feeling once again: *Why am I here again? What's wrong with these people?* We fail to realize that we're the only common denominator in all of these relationships.

Other ways in which the past shows up, of course, are in our experiences of guilt and shame and betrayal. Anxiety is common to the human condition. Anxiety is always anticipatory. It's always located in a possible future. Guilt and shame bind us to the past. They're rooted in the past. It's as if we are haunted by other images of ourselves. In Wakoski's poem, each family member has a painful history triggered by the photo. The speaker of the poem knows her only recourse is to get away, to flee, and she knows, as she sees herself in the mirror, the more she flees, the more she confirms her identification with that ancestral past that she wishes to repudiate. So we're haunted by an image of ourselves from the past.

Take guilt, for example. Guilt is something that I did or failed to do in the past. Anybody who's thoughtful at all will have areas of guilt. Some capacity to feel guilt is the only thing that makes us moral beings. A sociopath will feel no guilt, no remorse, and therefore has no real likelihood of altering behaviors because he can't see that it's a deplorable place in which to find oneself.

Then we also have contextual guilt. We in the Western world are often living at the expense of people in the developing worlds, and we know it. And often we feel an inauthentic sense of guilt too, where we think there's something wrong with us or we've done something wrong, when it's really a defense against anxiety. If a person feels a desire for a different kind of life, he or she may feel guilty about that rather than see that we are the vehicles of life's desire to seek expression. We will often shut the summons to being down and hedge it in. Guilt's a necessary emotion to have any sort of conscience whatsoever, and at the same time, obviously too much guilt is crippling.

SHAME AND BETRAYAL AS A SUMMONS TO CONSCIOUSNESS

About twenty-five years ago, I wrote the book *Swamplands of the Soul* dealing with such pleasant things as loss and betrayal and guilt. One person said, "Hey, you forgot shame." It occurred to me that in looking at about a dozen different kinds of swamplands that sooner or later we all find ourselves in, I'd wholly neglected shame.

Shame is not about what we did or didn't do. It's about two things: either a memory of where we failed to measure up to expectations or where we are subtly defined by our context. In other words, people can be shamed by poverty, shamed by alcoholism, shamed by abuse, shamed by racism and sexism, and so forth. When you ask, "What does that have to do with the soul of a child?" the answer is, of course, nothing, but again, the child doesn't know that. They get defined by that atmosphere, by that context. The insufficient reason and life experience of the child often lead to the fallacy: *I am what happened to me; I am my environmental message.*

I had to ask myself, *Why did I forget shame, and why did I fail to recognize its omnipresence in our lives?* Shame often shows up through our avoidances or our overcompensation or sometimes our grandiosity. When I reflected, I realized I and my family had grown up in shame. My family had been impoverished, unable to get any education or have any hope for any kind of better future. Their core message was "We don't expect these things. We don't deserve them. Let's huddle up and try to take care of each other as best we can." It was an understandable ethic of survival, but shame was what we had for cereal. It's no accident that I forgot shame in looking at the swampland. So I made a point, in subsequent books, including here, to be sure that I talk about shame because it is a possession by the past, by an absolute other that has been internalized by me, by the child, and stays in the adult's life as a kind of omnipresent gravitational pull downward into the swamp at all times.

Betrayal, too, is something that happens to all of us in life. It can be a summons to consciousness. How often has our failure to show up in our lives revealed an immaturity on our part, a failure to grow up, a collusion in victimhood? When we do that, we're betraying our own best selves. On the other hand, people have suffered grievous betrayals at times. In different decades and in different cities, I worked with two men whose stories were virtually identical. When they were approximately ten, they saw their mothers drive away with total strangers and never saw them again. Understandably, they had this profound sense of loss and betrayal. Each of them was in the process of unwittingly destroying their third marriage because, in each marriage, they refused to believe—or let us say, the psychic possession of the complex wouldn't allow them to believe—that this intimate other would not betray them too.

Each had gone to extreme lengths with polygraphs, tapping phones, and strategies of that sort to try to catch their wives in betrayal. Naturally the net effect of this was to drive their partners away, and understandably so. Each time, it was a confirmation: "See, there she goes again." But the "she" in that particular experience is really governed by the ancestral presence of that abandoning parent. What was so sad was this paranoid view recapitulated this history of loss. Paranoia is extrapolating a core fear to multiple other recipients, even those wholly undeserving. It's a form of "knowing" something—a believing something in the past and transferring it to the present and making it predictive of the future: *If she betrayed me, you will too, and I will look for enough evidence to prove that case and, in so doing, drive you away, and therefore, there's the proof.* This circular logic was a possession by the invisible powers and messages of the past.

There's also a collective sense of betrayal. People who have tried to do all the right things often, at midlife, will find themselves experiencing a depression or feeling a lack of satisfaction in what they're doing. Such moments feel like betrayals: *I did the best I could, I did what I was supposed to do, and why does it not work out? Why is it so difficult?*

Further, for some, there may be a cosmic sense of betrayal too. The poet Robert Frost wrote in his typical sardonic humor, "Forgive, O Lord, my little jokes on Thee / And I'll forgive Thy great big one on me."[5] Well, of course, the problem with betrayal is how and in what way people hang on to it and constantly go back to it. Therefore, they bind themselves to that disabling past and find it very difficult to move on.

Guilt and shame and betrayal are other forms of being possessed by the psychic past. There are so many things that go bump in the night, inform our actions and attitudes, and visibly move through the visible forms of our biographies.

Even nostalgia is an unconscious response to the betrayal of expectations. As we lose the fixed verities that we thought were the nature of nature or divinely given, we long for a past, and are thus possessed by an image of the past. The past wasn't so great. The past was based on social inequities, based on racism, based on sexism, based on the abuse of children, based on ignorance in positions of power. There's really not much to look forward to in going to the past because, again, it's a possession by an image of reality and not what the reality was. We have a kind of selective memory, even of our own experiences. We tend to romanticize childhood. From time to time, we have people with wonderful childhoods, but it was also a time of insecurity, of not knowing what was going on in the world, of fearing that one wouldn't have the sort of qualities or competency necessary for the tasks of life. Most children are anxious and nervous about how things are going and how they're going to manage it all. We tend to forget that when we look back on childhood.

THE HAUNTING OF OUR UNLIVED LIFE

There's another level, too, in which a culture can be possessed by the past. There's a kind of collective haunting that is troubling Western civilization. For example, many suffer a collective haunting of the lost gods. Jung asked the question, Where did the gods go when they left Olympus? It's a profound question.

We see faded institutional authority. We revisit their myths that linked our ancestors to the great four orders of meaning: the cosmos, nature, tribal identity, and selfhood. Those great narratives once linked and connected people to the invisible plane of reality that supports the visible plane of reality. Their absence leaves people chronically adrift and without points of guidance.

There are also hauntings that have come through the crimes that we have committed as people. I mentioned the ghetto at Kazimierz in Krakow as an example of our degradations against other human beings. Further, the destruction of Indigenous peoples around the world and our destruction of nature haunt our busy conscience. Nature is, of course, gathering its response in a way that's going to lead to a fateful reckoning for all of us.

We also have to acknowledge that the presence of the absences of the past is also a psychic haunting, that we're haunted by the lost sources of insight, connection, and links to transcendence. Recently I saw an author who said, "I don't believe in God anymore, but I sure do miss him." I thought that sentence was so telling about a profound nostalgia for a meaningful story and yet the person's present inability to affirm that story.

In our world, the de facto religion of materialism leads to this dilemma that we all have. If we don't encounter the numinous in the outer world and in the inner world, it will manifest itself as somatic illness for us or some form of pathology. Or we'll be owned by it in our search for it among the objects upon which we projected our existential yearning in the outer world. New shiny objects, seductive electronic technologies, sex and romance, hedonism, self-absorption, and most of all distraction by a noisy culture constitute the chief spirituality of our time. All are in some way compensatory to the experience of being haunted by a faded past, one that we can no longer access.

It requires each of us, then, to ask questions like: *Who am I apart from my history, my roles, my commitments?* It requires us to see the presence of what has continued to dictate for us, block us, direct us down this path instead of that path. Again, we must ask ourselves: *If I'm not here just to be adapted to the world that I receive, what am I here to serve and what wants to enter the world through me?*

That's dealing with what Jung calls "karma." Remember, karma works in different directions. We know that what we do or fail to do is going to influence our children and those who follow us, but it would be nice to think that at some level, our effort here could also perhaps work backward and relieve some of the burden of our ancestral history.

I want to share a client's dream in which this image and this possibility came up. He's out in nature, and suddenly a hawk sweeps down and seizes hold of his cheekbone with its talons. It's a terrifying experience. It's a visitation by a natural deity, so to speak, and he's staring directly eyeball to eyeball with this hawk.

"I gaze into the hawk's eyes, and I see unhappy spirits walking among the trees in single file. They are roped together and walk in silence, gloom, despair. At the front of the line are my parents, and behind them are their parents and parents going back in time. The hawk tells me that I must loosen the rope that binds them. I tell the hawk I do not know how to do this, but the hawk bestows a feather on me and tells me I have one life to live in which to free these spirits, and do not forget those spirits need you."

That's a very profound dream. It was sort of like the famous statue by Auguste Rodin of the Burghers of Calais in which the city council of Calais was roped together by an invader and threatened to be murdered on behalf of the city in lieu of a ransom. Remember that the image of his ancestral line and his psychological work was not created by his ego; it came from the Self. The Self apparently was saying, *The work you're doing here is touching deeply not only your present life but well into this ancestral lineage also.*

Of all of our hauntings, the most devastating arise from our unlived life—the life that we're carrying within us as a possibility and as a service to the universe and others. The wisdom of nature and of our ancestors courses through all of us. There are also archetypal forces seeking renewal. Sometimes we have to ask the question of ourselves directly: *Do I have a soul, however I understand that word* soul? *And if I do, what is it asking of me?* That's an intimidating question but a necessary summons to consider from time to time.

Back when he was an undergraduate, Jung gave a series of lectures at a debate society in around 1895. In one of them, he already noted the reluctance of his contemporaries to listen to the voices of the inner life; they preferred to be distracted by the clamorous controversies of the outer world. He even hated the dictatorial powers of the telephone to interrupt one's life and demand response. What would he have thought of our modern wired culture of 24/7 linkage to outer noise and distraction?

Jung was aware of our aversion to dialogue with our own souls long before Home Shopping Network and Twitter and TikTok and the blandishments of modern culture, that's for sure. Despite these spectral presences—the haunting of griefs, betrayals, and blocking agencies—we still have a job in life, and that's to show up as best we can. Over and over I've seen really fine people who express a general malaise, an indefinable desire for something different. Their job is okay, their marriage is okay, their relationship to life is okay, but then again, it's not.

When one starts to push against that malaise, one hears over and over, *But that's just the way I am.* Or, *I'm too old to change now, because I'm too near retirement, we don't have the money, the kids wouldn't understand,* and so on. All of those outer facts might be true, but psychological mischief is almost always never about what it's about.

Sooner or later, the real issue will be found in the complexes, those affect-laden ideas, those acquired messages that stand in the way of our growth even now. If we can pull apart those blocking messages, we see a learned helplessness, an idea deeply reinforced in our history, a reticulated admonishment with which we remain stuck in stasis with its attending calculus of costs.

We know life is always more powerful, more imposing, more intractable than any of us can consciously manage. And still we're asked to show up. Wakoski concluded her poem, "How I hate my destiny."[6] Again, I don't know if she meant destiny or fate, but if it was destiny, she's in a sense confessing that "I'm defined by that history and unable to do anything about it."

I would hate to think that is the case. Maybe the act of writing the poem was an effort to work some of that through. But it's so clear: That past is not past; it's still operative. How is it operative? That very pragmatic question might help discernment: *What does it make me do? What does it keep me from doing?* We need to be, in a healthy way, ghost busters for the rest of our lives or, if we're not going to deal with them and banish them to the past, at least make peace with them. We live in haunted houses and sleep in memory's unmade bed.

6

Finding Personal Resilience
in Times of Change

I n this chapter, we're going to explore the times of in-between, which we all experience periodically on both personal and cultural levels. Often in the tides of human affairs (what we call history) and, of course, in the tides of personal life (what we often call crisis), we find ourselves in between, perhaps between what we thought we knew, what we thought we understood, and what we thought was a reliable map of our world and that now seems to fail us. This idea of the in-between turned out to be the inspiration for an entire book, so you'll find some overlap between this chapter and a deeper exploration of the topic in *Living Between Worlds*.

TIMES OF IN-BETWEEN

Among many of my patients I have found something spent, finished, played out, exhausted, dead, and something not yet apparent, still over the horizon, perhaps not even there. These in-between times come also in the tides of history. For example, over two millennia ago, a terrible rumor spread around the Mediterranean that Pan had died, and it caused "panic." Now maybe that news failed to move you, but you've been influenced by it whether you know it or not.

Pan, the son of Hermes, was the only god who is known to die. He was the god of nature, sexuality, instinctual life, and the vegetal world; and his death signaled the shifting of authority from instinctual and natural being to theology, morality, institutionalization, and often neurosis. Neurosis is what rises out of the conflict between our instinctual realities and our cultural claims upon us. As Freud pointed out so succinctly, the price of civilization is neurosis. However, Pan was not apparently the only mortal god, so to speak (which is an oxymoron). Many sensitive observers in the nineteenth century also felt the slippage of firm ground. Matthew Arnold, the son of the famous Thomas Arnold, who was one of the great church leaders, wrote in "Stanzas from the Grande Chartreuse," "Wandering between two worlds, one dead / The other powerless to be born."[1]

All of us recognize we're in an in-between time in our culture when certain verities, or presumed verities, have lost their authority and compelling power. Powerful forces are at loose in the world, the direction of which and the outcome of which are very much up for grabs. We sense it also in Matthew Arnold's famous poem "Dover Beach," where he furthers that slippage. He said,

The Sea of Faith
Was once, too, at the full and round earth's shore
Lay like the folds of a bright girdle furled.
But now I only hear
Its melancholy, long, withdrawing roar,
Retreating, to the breath
Of the night-wind, down the vast edges drear
And naked shingles of the world.[2]

In the last stanza of that poem, he turns to his wife and says, essentially, we have to cling to each other; we're all that we can count on. The world that we thought we were going to enter seems to be slipping away from us. Moreover, he concludes by noting they live between ignorant armies clashing by night. It's often thought that those ignorant armies he was alluding to were the partisans of the religious orthodoxy and the new sciences, as unfolded in the famous "monkey debates" between Bishop Samuel Wilberforce and Thomas Huxley and so forth. The inflamed contentiousness that arose out of that conflict is still very much in our culture's discontent.

The famous novelist George Eliot talked about how three great ideas have animated humankind: God, immortality, and duty. She says how unbelievable the first two are now to her—God and immortality—but duty remains. That's the classic Victorian dilemma: you've removed the metaphysical superstructure, but you still have duty.

In 1882, in *The Joyful Science*, Nietzsche proclaims the death of God and that the slayer of God was us through our routinization, enervated rituals, and so forth. Dostoevsky added that without God, all things are possible—all things. So we've taken on the powers of the gods, as we know, split the atom, loosed the nuclear genie, and as William Butler Yeats so memorably spoke in the last century, "Now days are dragon-ridden, the nightmare / Rides upon sleep."[3]

THE LOSS OF THE NUMINOUS

When I was in school in the 1970s, I came across this paragraph from Jung, and without knowing it at the time, it changed my life.

He said,

> We think we can congratulate ourselves on having already reached such a pinnacle of clarity, imagining that we have left all these phantasmal gods far behind. But what we have left behind are only verbal spectres, not the psychic facts that were responsible for the birth of the gods. We are still as much possessed by autonomous psychic contents as if they were Olympians. Today they are called phobias, obsessions, and so forth; in a word, neurotic symptoms. The gods have become diseases; Zeus no longer rules Olympus but rather the solar plexus, and produces curious specimens for the doctor's consulting room, or disorders the brains of politicians and journalists who unwittingly let loose psychic epidemics on the world.[4]

That paragraph helped me understand my confusions, the perduring split between my tradition and my emotional reality, the growing crevasse within between wish and reality. It led to my thesis and ultimately to the book *Tracking the Gods*. If the gods have left Olympus, where have they gone? The gods are personified energies that course through the cosmos; although from time to time, they inhabit a certain concept, a certain belief, a certain structure, but then, because they are godly, they depart and go elsewhere. Therefore, our task is to track those energies and identify in what new form they make their appearance.

Let's unpack Jung's paragraph above. First, when we talk about myth, we think of myth as other people's religion, not mine—which is the truth, of course. One of our closet beliefs is that our complex-driven rationality is capable of discernment—a grasping of truth that's denied to others. Therefore, in our primitivity, we are shielded from the irony that our historic condescension will someday be similarly viewed with condescension by those who replace us.

Second, a "god" is encountered whenever one is engaged by the Wholly Other. The other, which is transcendent to our ego-complex sense of reality, is the primary phenomenon.

Third, the ego attaches to the epiphenomenon, which is the secondary image rising out of such encounters with the Wholly Other, rather than the energy, which gave rise to and animated that image in the first place. Our ego state desires the predictable, the knowable, the manageable, and therefore grows bewitched by the image, not the autonomous invisible energy that infused that tangible image with luminosity.

I had a client years ago who, as he got older, wanted to revisit some of the religious beliefs that he had as a child, ones he'd left behind a long time ago. He joined a Bible study group in his community, and he had a dream that took place in the middle of a group discussion. In the dream, he said, "You have to realize that what is sacred is not the light bulb but the energy that infuses the bulb with light. When the energy is depleted, the bulb is left behind." In the dream, someone condemns him for such an idea. (Most likely, that condemnation came from a part of himself that was not wanting quite to take that step.)

I said to him, "Your psyche perhaps solved this problem for you." What is really divine is the energy moving invisibly through the universe and through us. It is not necessarily the vehicle or the husk that it occupies at any given moment. My body, a husk, is not immortal, but possibly the spirit that informs and animates it might be.

Returning to Jung's words above, we never know phenomena or things in themselves but only our subjective experience of them. So, metaphysical theology has tended to be replaced by phenomenology and subjective descriptions of intrapsychic experience. In other words, not *What is the other?* but *How do I experience it, and how does my subjective process alter and change it?*

For example, there was a time when the concept of Zeus was charged with that luminous energy. Today, it's only a concept, moving neither heart nor mind. Still, the ego is often bewitched by the literalism of confusing the name Zeus with the energy that once animated it.

The bright crew on Olympus has left and relocated, though the husk of their presence remains. Given Jung's definition of a neurosis as a neglected or repressed god, we're still at the mercy of those energies, which were once embodied as those shining presences atop Olympus.

Today, rather than say we are possessed by Aphrodite or abandoned by her, we can purchase a self-help book on love's disorders and perhaps acquire five easy steps for her retrieval. Or rather than saying we're in the grip of mad Ares, we feel inflamed by righteous anger and justify the right to attack our neighbor, and so on.

Finally, on the personal level, we suffer neuroses. In an age of great material access, we increasingly experience an emptiness, an anomie, aimlessness—all illnesses of the soul. On a collective level, our treatment plans for the absence of the gods are materialism, hedonism, narcissism, nationalism, and a coursing nostalgia for a world that never really existed.

MYTHS LINK US TO THE MYSTERIES

We all are summoned to a heroic journey, but our contemporary odysseys are redirected to the Apple store, the palliative pharmacy, or forays along the river Amazon Prime. Guided by Google whereby all things are available, we wonder why we're so absent-spirited, so lost, so adrift. We may say that these "isms" constitute our values, our de facto religions, those in which we invest our energies. Then we have to ask the obvious question: How well are they working for us? To what zones transcendent do they link us?

The American poet Archibald MacLeish put it succinctly: "A world ends when its metaphor has died."[5] So where are we, then, today, in this in-between state? Something clearly has ended. Despite the horrific bloodshed of World Wars I and II, the great historic destructions of famine, plague, and war, which have haunted humankind, have largely been contained in most parts of the world. Moreover, they are no longer seen as driven by the gods but proved manageable problems if we're wise enough and disciplined in our approach to them. No longer are we here to serve the monarch or God's representative on earth, but they're here to serve us, to make the conditions of life more congenial to our greatest fantasized goal: abiding happiness.

Today, through life extension and achieving living conditions that our ancestors would've surely thought would produce happiness, we have moved into those realms once reserved for the gods. And so, how happy are we? As one character says to another in *Waiting for Godot*, "We're happy! What do we do now, now that we are happy?"[6] How do we fill our hours until the chap with a scythe shows up? Well, our popular culture's answer to that seems to be divertissement: diversion, sensation piled on sensation, with an admixture of violence.

From childhood on, I placed my chips on the fantasy of education, not only to rescue me but to save our age. Moreover, I've spent my entire adult life as an educator, and yet our level of education is deplorable. Despite all the evidence of the antiquity of this planet, nearly 50 percent of Americans believe that God created humans in their present form within the last four thousand years. So much for the dinosaur bones and other evidence of human existence stretching further and further back in time.

With fervor, many defend creationism, even though it's full of gaps and contradictions. Why? Here, Jung's concept of complexes is helpful. It's far scarier to imagine a universe driven by algorithms and impersonal forces than to project a parental imago on the vast cosmos that serves the fantasy that something or someone better be in charge and something better be purposely unfolding.

Recently more than one person has asked me, how can we continue to live in a time such as ours, a time of cynicism, corruption, and the degradation of values we hold dear? And the answer is simple: How can we not? All ages have their problems, and most of ours are first-world problems. Most of us have grown to take food and shelter and relative security for granted. In fact, our life is so much easier than that of our ancestors. Yet we are in a time of cultural confusion, paradigm shifts, and anxiety-generating in-between times. The place to which all of us have to come is basically this: you are defined by what lies most deeply within you, by your values, and by your actions. The acts of others, especially those who are disordered, do not define you. Civilization has always depended on the good people doing what is necessary for the daily maintenance of their society.

Children are comforted, classes are held, hospitals open their doors, and so on. We all have a personal and a social service to do in the healing of our time. Perhaps the question is better framed: How can I live without my myth? How can I live in this great in-between that comes to all civilizations and to each of us from time to time? Of course, by *myth*, I'm not using the word as synonymous with falsehood. I mean it in a sense of energy-laden images that are capable of moving our spirits and our souls. Historically, the purpose of myth was to link people to the mysteries in meaningful and felt ways.

The first mystery is that of the nature of the cosmos: Is this a "cosmos," an ordered universe, or is it chaotic? If so, what are those organizing principles, and what is our role in it? Second is the mystery of nature: How do we live in beneficent relationship with nature rather than be the devouring destructive presence as we have been? The third mystery touches our social identity: Who is my tribe, to whom do I belong, where is my home, who are my people, and how do we answer that question today? Finally, the mystery of individual selfhood: Who am I, what is my journey, how is it different from someone else's, and how am I to find my way?

Those questions historically were framed by the great stories of tribal experience. As those stories have eroded in their powers to connect, individuals have been thrown back upon the abyss of the psyche. Jung put it once in a letter where he said that the modern fell off the roof of the medieval cathedral into the abyss of the self. So, how do we navigate our way then?

SOMETHING BIGGER THAN OURSELVES

In the civilizations preceding us, most people believed there was a cosmic plan, an enfolding and unfolding energy of which they were a part. If a sparrow fell, it was part of God's plan as were death, disease, and famine. While humans might have had attitudes about those forces, they didn't question the implacability of those forces. The key was to live in accord with the will of the gods—as best one could figure that out. Don't espouse that thought, don't cross this line, be humble and trust. But today, if a child dies of a disease, we expect the Centers for Disease Control and Prevention to exercise vigilance in apprehending the viral visitor that encroached our world and plan a repellent. If a plane falls from the sky, we expect the National Transportation and Safety Board to figure out why and correct it before my plane takes off.

Though their physics, archaeology, and geology are two thousand to four thousand years old, even the most rabid fundamentalists today would never walk into the ER and say, "I want to only be given the treatment available to Moses or Jesus or Mohammed, and of course don't bother about that anesthetic stuff. And while I'm here, why not trepan my brain and let all those evil spirits out." In other words, at that moment, they shift to wanting the best palliatives contemporary science can provide.

Our minds and our methods have produced wondrous accomplishments over the last few centuries, but there may be a price for all this advance. In his book *Homo Deus: A Brief History of Tomorrow*, Yuval Noah Harari notes that humans agree to give up meaning in exchange for power. That's a very loaded idea. In other words, we are presumably no longer actors in a cosmic script but the uncertain engineers of our own fate. In the postmodern myth, there is no cosmic script, no happy ending, nothing inherently to give meaning.

The science fiction writer Vernor Vinge popularized the idea of what he called the "Singularity" in his 1993 essay "Technological Singularity." He described this phenomenon as a tipping point, a moment when the old paradigm no longer works, when a new order is moving and shaping events whether people at the time know it or not. We can say that the utilization of fire, the discovery of tools, and the emergence of machines were such moments in history. In our time, the ubiquitous computer is the outer manifestation of the movement into artificial intelligence through the infinite variety of binary, off-and-on combinations. Think how recently this world arrived and how hard it is to imagine living without the computer. The real "Singularity," however, will arise when that tool is capable of outthinking us, of critiquing its own moves. We call consciousness the capacity to reflect on our reflections. The computer world is very near, if not already arrived, at this capacity as well. What the implications are of this shift from nature to a world artificially created, which then has the power to critique the denizens of that natural world who created it, is anyone's guess. Such change introduces a world of ambiguity, and humankind has never tolerated ambiguity very well.

We're right at the edge of that, if not already in that world. What will it mean when the machines think better than we do? Imagine better than we do? It's not enough to say, *Well, they'll never be creative like us.* We've been saying that for a long time, and increasingly evidence accumulates to suggest the opposite. (AI is now writing novels, creating works of art, and challenging us to discern that the origins of each are nonhuman.) The reason I mention this is because this is one of the great psychosocial-mythological shifts that we're all going through. And no one knows where it's going. We all have those questions: Where are we going? Where am I going? How do I find my way?

In his personal life, Jung asked that question like everybody else, and he started with his family of origin. When he asked his father, the cleric, about large questions, he got in response, "Only believe; believe our tradition." When he asked his mother, he got a séance, a magic channel, in return. When he finally left home and went into the world, he concluded that the words that most characterized his parental influences were the "powerlessness" of his father and the "unreliability" of his mother. So it's no wonder he had to find another path. He concluded that within each of us, there is some locus of knowing, independent of ego consciousness, a center that produces our dreams to correct us, symptoms to challenge us, and visions to inspire us. His was not an amateur's trust in impulse or captivation by complex. It was a long, patient humbling attendance upon the psyche or soul and its many perspicacious permutations.

In a 1939 speech in London, Jung noted that absent a sense of connection to something numinous, we have to create disturbances. Speaking of that troubled hour before the great conflagration, Jung noted that, paradoxically, many would welcome war because at last they could live in relationship to something bigger than themselves. Of course, that war was imminently upon them and nearly destroyed everything.

That need for the distraction from ourselves reminds me of that passage in Albert Camus's novel *The Fall*, in which he talks about how wonderful it is for the neighborhood to have a murder because there's something to lift one out of the horizontal, to give one something to talk about, to gossip about. It's something happening, something bigger than ourselves. Jung's concept of "something bigger than ourselves" reveals our deep, deep hunger for more than the ego-bound world. (Remember those pilgrimages to the casinos as another example.)

To live in the postmodern world is not just to be alive and breathing; it's to understand that the gift and burden of meaning has shifted from tribal mythology and sacred institution to the individual. In 1862, Emily Dickinson, in a letter to the poet Thomas Higginson, wrote a very interesting aphorism, which has struck my fancy. She said, "The Sailor cannot see the North, but knows the Needle can."[7] She was a young struggling poet in Amherst, Massachusetts—a tiny village at the time. She wrote to the published poet in Boston, asking Higginson his opinion of the sheath of poems that she had sent him. He wrote a letter in response that was polite but condescending, telling her she had a lot of work yet to do and so forth. She took all that in and wrote back a polite letter, thanking him for his time and comments, and then added that aphorism: "The Sailor cannot see the North, but knows the Needle can."

What we see in her work is a person who, as a premodern "modern," recognized the shift of authority from the group and sacred institutions to the individual, and the necessity of each person finding a compass. I think what she was saying was, *I take in your comments and criticism, but I also believe in what I'm working toward.* This was a woman who at a young age scandalized her family and her village for the rest of her life by ceasing to go to religious services. Many of her poems raised profound questions about the nature of the universe; they're explosive in their messages. But all in all, she was acutely aware of that psychosocial shift and the need for an internal compass.

RIGHT RELATIONSHIP TO OUR SOUL

For some, the gift of an internal compass is an intolerable threat, and people retreat into a dogmatic defiance or perhaps into a drug-addled deflection. But for others of us, it can be an invitation to a life of dignity, of responsibility, and the possibility of great meaning.

Just a few years after Jung's speech in London, Christopher Fry wrote *A Sleep of Prisoners*, a play in which he said, "Dark and cold we may be, but this is no winter now. The frozen misery of centuries breaks, cracks, begins to move. The thunder is the thunder of the flows, the thaw, the flood, the upstart spring. Thank God our time is now when wrong comes up to face us everywhere, never to leave us till we take the longest stride of soul we ever took. Affairs are now soul size. The enterprise is exploration into God. So what are you waiting for? It takes so many thousand years to wake, but will you wake for pity's sake?"[8]

Fry addresses things so beautifully in that sentence: "Affairs are now soul size." It raises that elemental question (however you understand the word *soul*): Do I have a soul? And if so, what is it asking of me? How do I honor that? In a prior chapter, I told you about that peculiar encounter I experienced in the Atlantic City casino where I was asked the question, Where is my home? I disassociated and reflected on the archetypal value, prominence, and necessity of asking that question. What came up for me from the depths, the intrapsychic depths, was that today, for me and for many of us, our home is our journey. Our journey is framed by our questions. Our journey is found in our explorations. There's no home to return to because that ultimately is a regression. There is no Valhalla out there to attain; there's the journey itself.

Today I can understand what I could not as a child: that the journey is our home. You may know and love the poem "Ithaca" by Greek poet C. P. Cavafy. He imagines what Odysseus might feel as he finally is able to pull back into his home harbor after ten years of bloodletting on the plains of Troy and ten years on the wine-dark sea. He offers some advice, whispers in the ear of Odysseus, and says to him to keep his Ithaca in his vision but to realize that Ithaca itself is not the goal. The search for Ithaca has given him the rich, tumultuous journey. His affirmation of that invitation is why today we honor Odysseus, even as we are summoned to undertake our own journeys into the unknown.

We all best live times in-between when we live the journey as fully as we can, engaging both the sirens of the thousand seductive distractions our world makes available to us and the sea serpents with their intimidations as they arise from the spindrift of our lives. Guided by natural curiosity and longing, we too may drop our plumb line into those same guiding currents that ran through the souls of the ancients and run through all of ours as well.

One of the things that's become increasingly clear to me through the years of personal work, but also from working with the psyche of others, day in and day out, hour by hour, is something within us knows us better than we know ourselves. Something in us, each of us, knows what's right for us. Something in us contains the wisdom of nature, the wisdom of the ages, even though we may have lost contact with it. Something within us is trying to communicate with us, and it only makes sense to stop and pay attention.

Again, the word *therapy* comes from *therapeuein*: to listen or attend to psyche, the soul. What does it mean to listen to the soul and attend to it? To respect the fact that we have these autonomous feeling responses to our life? While we've learned to suppress them and anesthetize them, they are nonetheless qualitative analyses undertaken autonomously by the psyche to tell us of its approval or disapproval. Notice that we have various energy systems, and when we are in right relationship to our own soul, the energy is there. It supports us. We lose ourselves; we get in the zone, we say. Time disappears, and we feel the rightness of things.

Other times, when we continue to push against the stream and we continue to bark up the wrong tree, we find ultimately the energy drained, and we find ourselves enervated, distracted, depressed. We also have the presence of dreams even when we don't pay attention to them. But when we do, we begin to realize something there speaks so clearly and invites our dialogue.

LIFE HAS NOT FORGOTTEN YOU

I recall being in the fourth year of my own analytic process, which was a considerable investment of time and money and soul energy, and walking out of an analytic session after having had one more dream speak the same thing. I realized that the proverbial feather had tilted the whole balance intrapsychically. My personal conundrums shifted in that moment from a thought of the head to a felt experience of the heart. In that acceptance and realization, I said something like, "Holy cow! There is a Self; there is a self with a capital S. There is a soul, and it's speaking, and it has been speaking." It had been speaking for a very long time, and it first showed up in those irritations we call "symptoms"—a loss of energy, a depression.

The more we flail and continue to employ the strategies of the past, the deeper the hole gets. Then we begin to realize that something else is calling for accountability. We're called back to an interior council, and it's time to shut up and pay attention and to ask, what is the soul wanting of us? What we've construed in contemporary times is a vast system of distraction. This is not new; it's simply ramped up. All of the noise and flimflam of the hour is designed to distract, amuse, obscure the deeper dimensions of our lives.

In the seventeenth century, Blaise Pascal, in his book *Pensées* (Thoughts), said even the king, king though he be, if he thinks of self will grow miserable and frightened. So the court has invented the Jester to distract the king and the court from reflecting on things that matter. Pascal labeled this distraction "divertissement," what we now call "diversion." Think about that in the light of contemporary culture with its twenty-four-hour seven-days-a-week wired-in experience of distraction.

So much greater must be our estrangement from our own souls. So much greater must be our fear of that still, quiet voice that speaks within each of us. The ancients knew this voice, and they talked about it. They chronicled it. They wrote scripture and mythologies about it. And then we forgot what they learned. The question is, can we return to that? This whole process of stepping into our own depths can be intimidating. It can feel isolating, and still, we have to remember, this is our journey. This risk is what brings depth and dignity to our lives.

Let's turn once again to a paragraph from Rainer Maria Rilke's fine *Letters to a Young Poet*. When the young poet is expressing his apprehensions about the difficulties of life and whether he'll be up to it or not, Rilke writes to him,

"You must not be frightened if a sadness rises up before you larger than you've ever seen, if a restiveness like light and cloud shadows pass over your hands and over all you do, you must think that something is happening with you. That life has not forgotten you, that it holds you in its hand. It will not let you fall. Why do you want to shut out of your life any uneasiness? Any miseries or any depressions? For, after all, you do not know what work these conditions are doing for you."[9]

It's a lovely paragraph because it's a reminder that there's something in us, a life force that supports us, that holds us in its hand. Rilke also wrote the lovely poem "*Herbst*," or "Autumn." In it he notes the falling leaves and realizes that all things are falling. Even this heavy earth on which we stand is falling through time and space, and the poem builds on the metaphor of all things falling. He says, and yet there is that which in its hands gently holds this falling endlessly. On a cosmic level, he could say that it is a cosmic spirit like God. On the personal level, he could talk about that as the archetype of the Self, which is that which provides us continuity and the undergirding of our nature to support us in difficult times.

Remember Rilke wrote, and I touched on this previously, our task is to continuously fail at ever larger things. Again, our youthful ego says, *Fail? I don't want to fail.* But then when we think about ever larger things, it means the soul is on its journey. And so in times in-between, we all have to find our own guiding centers, and the journey and the locus of those centers will vary for each of us. For the last few centuries, it's become clearer and clearer that those are to be found within and not outside of us in tribal myth, in residual institutions, or received authorities.

None of this is an undermining of or flight from the community. A society is organized to serve a purpose, but it's very fragile, easily disintegrates, and lacks a core. Community often is found ironically in the meeting of those who've undertaken a journey—a journey seeking some forms of consciousness, some forms of awareness, and some willingness to submit themselves to a process that is less invested in ego security and the fixities of knowledge that we think our ancestors had, but rather in the unfolding discoveries of those journeys. Our own psyche keeps showing up, keeps knocking on the door, keeps summoning us back to the high calling of the journey.

This is important because the soul also provides each of us the tools with which to navigate and constantly reminds us that we're charged from the beginning with accountability to what may be seeking its expression through us into the world. Our psyche is constantly summoning us, calling us back to the higher calling of that journey. Moreover, it gives us the tools with which to navigate, to find our way—the internal compass. It reminds us from time to time that we are charged from the beginning of the journey to its end with accountability to what is seeking its expression through us into the world, asking us only that we manage to be as courageous as possible, to show up as best we can, and to live that journey with as much integrity as we can muster.

THE WORK OF FINDING OUR COMPASS

This work of finding our compass and attending to it involves a measure of discipline, to be sure. Every day we need to check in with our own souls, to pull out of the melee of our journey, the noisy distractions, the necessary duties, and to say, "What's going on here?"

My friend and colleague Marion Woodman once asked people before they began therapy with her, to agree to devote one full hour every day to working with a journal, practicing active imagination, and working with dreams. She said, many people said, "But I don't have that kind of time. I can't cut that out of my schedule," to which she respectfully responded, "Then you're not serious about this work. What could be more important than this kind of encounter with the magnitude of your own soul's journey?"[10]

I want to emphasize the magnitude of the soul's journey because it does intimidate us. We've all seen how a baby starts to cry the moment it loses contact with the parent. I have a colleague who has twins, and he notices how every once in a while, one of the twins will just walk over and touch the body of the other twin to sort of reassure themselves, *Ah, you're still there*. So, we have some sense of the fear of disconnect of being out there on our own.

I remember visiting the National Air and Space Museum in Washington, DC, in the Smithsonian Collection, and watching the first walk in space. Of course I had seen it on television at the time it happened, but as that astronaut stepped out from the "mothership" into empty space, held there only by that thin tether, something in me just rippled with, I will call it, existential anxiety.

I thought, *What happens if that tether breaks?* Of course, that was a subject of a movie years later. I realized in that image the magnitude and the power of our need to stay connected. This need is found even in the word *religion*, which etymologically suggests reconnecting with that separated Other. We all have dependency needs, but when they prevail, one misses out in finding the resources that life has also given us. For this reason, I agree with Woodman, that every day some time needs to be set aside, perhaps in the morning, perhaps at night, to formally address the workings of one's psychic life. This can show up through journaling, which is important, because you don't sit down and say into the journal, "Dear Diary, this is what happened today." More important is to ask: What got touched today? What generated a significant amount of energy? Where did that energy come from? What did that touch in my history? What satellite issues might that have activated?

Perhaps we had some conflict with someone in the course of the day that continues to reverberate for us. We pursue that resonance. We can ask, Where does this come from in my history? It's easy to dismiss it as only something that happened "out there." But we might find that pursuing it stirs resonant rings of influence such as of the fear of conflict or in the difficulty of being able to hold our own in the presence of a large other. So, when journaling, ask, What got touched today? What was that about? Where did that activate some aspect of my history? What do I need to know about that? How do I need to bring the wherewithal of my modern adult capacity to that arena?

Earlier I indicated that stuck places are always defenses against anxiety. The anxiety usually is an archaic anxiety. It's there from long ago and far away. And yet because it's there in the basement and gets activated, it has the power to come up and shut us down. That's what keeps us stuck, even if there's a part of us that's separate and says, *I'm stuck here, and I want to get beyond this.* Then what is required of us is confronting that anxiety and finding in that anxiety what the specific fears are. The fears always come down to either feeling the overwhelment of others or of the world's demands or the loss of connection with others or the world. Those are our fears of overwhelment and abandonment again. Sooner or later, our anxiety always tracks back to those two categories of threat. As we pay attention in our journal, we recognize that it doesn't have to be entered every day. We turn to it when something occurs.

Often when people are driving away from a session, their best thought appears. That's because the material has been activated. Sometimes they wake up with it at 3:00 the next morning. I always say, "Pay attention to those waking thoughts." Some of them are tied to our specific daily anxieties, yes. But they are things that have been triggered, and we need to figure out what has been catalyzed and why.

THE TECHNIQUE OF ACTIVE IMAGINATION

From time to time, we also need to employ the technique of active imagination. Jung developed this in a profound way. Active imagination is not meditation, and it's not guided imagery. Those are other kinds of techniques. This process, as suggested in the name, is "activating the image."

Let's say, for example, I dream that I'm in a house or a strange place where there's a sinister presence, and I think someone is trying to kill me or is hostile toward me. I wake up in an anxious state. Of course, from the ego standpoint, the most natural thing for me to do is get out of that house, to forget the dream, ignore it.

Rather, I have to ask myself, *Why has this dream come?* Dreams are not arbitrary. They're not planted in our brain by alien forces. They are natural by-products of our psyche seeking its own healing and development. That's the thing you need to remember. Dreams come to us as part of the psyche's natural process of healing itself or developing our journey.

So I ask myself, *What is this presence, this sinister threat?* Then I go back into that dream. I find a quiet place, not interrupted by the telephone or noisy traffic outside, and reenter the psychic space of the dream—the last thing the ego would normally want to do. Yet the dream is a product of my own nature. So why should I be estranged from my own nature? So, I enter that room, that space, and I approach that person. I say, "Who are you? Why are you here? What do you want from me?"

You'd be surprised. Maybe the first couple of times you try active imagination, you will feel as if nothing happened because the ego is still clinging to its conventional sense of reality. It doesn't want to be in that room, or it says, *Oh, I'm just making this stuff up.* I've had those reactions as well. But as you practice, you begin to realize you can slip more easily into a subjective experience of that setting. Out of that often comes the revelation that the energy may be something that we have split off and its ostensible anger toward us is seeking our love, our healing, our reenergization. Or it allows us to recognize that perhaps there are certain forces that are dangerous in our environment and that we need to pay more attention to them.

You will recall that my own analytic work in Zurich began with a dream of an imperiled knight on the ramparts of a castle that was under siege. The siege was being directed by a witchlike figure at the edge of the forest, and the dream ended with an enormous amount of anxiety about whether the castle will hold. My analyst said, "We're going to have to lower the drawbridge and go out and meet her and see why she's so angry with you." You may imagine my ambivalence: Fear piped up and immediately protested, "Are you kidding? She's trying to kill me." And yet I thought, *I'm here; I've come this far; this is the work.*

We engaged in an active imagination in that first session. I went back into that space, and she motioned me into the forest. In the forest, she opened a large book that was full of strange symbols, like hieroglyphics. After that, the "interior movie" shut down. But I realized what she was really saying to me was, "You are invited to encounter the mysteries here. You are invited to a process that's going to take you the rest of your life, but it's going to make your life more and more interesting than it ever was."

From the standpoint of street logic, our outer sense of reality may think, *Oh, what nonsense is this? You know, we're just making up talk in our head.* But here's the thing to remember: The psyche is unconscious. It is energy systems at work, and it only becomes conscious when it activates or embodies itself through an image, such as a dream image or a behavioral-pattern image. In that moment, I can make something of that invisible world visible. So by activating the image, which is what is meant by active imagination, I allow it, from an ego standpoint, autonomy. I'm not there to control it. But I may begin to converse with it.

That's why I'm not particularly a believer in or an advocate of so-called lucid dreaming, if such is possible, where people try to enter their dreams and change the ending, because that's defeating the whole purpose. That's the ego reasserting its sovereignty rather than saying, "Why has the psyche spoken to me in this way? What does it wish to tell me? What do I need to learn here? Perhaps where do I need to be humbled in order to do that?" So the whole notion of lucid dreaming is contrary to soliciting the wisdom of our nature. It's seeking to control it one more time, one more subtle way.

My first active imagination, in the contested field of the anima—which is the interior world of feeling life, instinctual life, and spiritual life—was saying, *You're at the beginning of a journey, and you're going to explore mysteries that you wouldn't have guessed. It's going to be a very interesting journey.* How could I, under the circumstances, refuse to take it, given that kind of invitation? There are subsequent ways in which I undertook a conversation with that witch figure until she eventually transformed into a beautiful presence.

I guess I should tell you the end of that story. Years later, in the last dream I had before leaving Zürich and returning to America, I found myself under an arching entrance into, of all places, the estate of Elvis Presley in Memphis, Tennessee. As you may recall, that estate is called Graceland. I'd never been there. A feminine presence, which by then was more familiar to me, came out of the mansion and down a curving walkway with her arms full of rose petals. She came up to me, smiled, and handed me a handful of rose petals and then walked on.

It was an encounter of the goddess, so to speak. The witch had been transformed into a beautiful presence. My analyst leaned back and said, "Well, I think our work has been worth it." And indeed, it was. That wasn't the end of the journey, but it was certainly the end of a significant phase of the journey, a journey begun in the grip of what was called "the dark damsel," manifesting as a midlife depression. The depression lifted and a new avenue of life opened.

Active imagination and dream work are forms of paying attention to and listening to the psyche as it manifests. There, we begin to realize that the Self is transcendent to ordinary ego consciousness and is seeking to connect with us with the wisdom of nature. It is not necessarily going to fit into the conventional intelligence of our culture with which we must deal every day, but it is something that is larger than this time and this place. It is willing to risk its investment in us. How dare we, then, not undertake a journey that is seeking its expression through us?

When we do this, it's a humbling process, but it gives a profound sense of personal purpose, depth, and dignity to our journey. No amount of outer accomplishments or recognition by the world ever equals that inner conviction—the conviction that one is living one's journey as honestly and as faithfully as one can. All of us, I believe, are invited to that journey, and all of us are naturally equipped for it. We can thank depth psychology, and specifically the work of Jung, for giving us some of these tools with which to address it. When we do, we will find that the wisdom of the ancients is, once again, available to each of us.

7

Reviewing the Journey

In this chapter, we're going to look at our later years. If you are still very early in the process, this may appear remote, but trust me, it's headed your way. For others, it will be a reminder of how we need to periodically review our lives by asking: What has it been about? What is this journey about really? As you know, in the first half of life, we're mostly responding to demands placed on us by parents, schoolteachers, peers, partners, bosses, and so forth. The second half of life is quite a different agenda where we have to try to figure out what this life really means, why we are here, and to what we are in service. In this chapter, I'll offer some ideas and thoughts about the later years and the process of reviewing your life.

When I was young, sixty was old and sixty-five was dead. Yes, I knew people who were in their seventies, but very, very few of them; and even fewer ever reached eighty. We all know that statistic has changed dramatically. Today, the average length of life in North America is now hovering near eighty. We think of a person who dies in their seventies as having died early. Historians tell us that in the classical era, the average length of life was probably in the middle twenties. In 1900, it was only forty-seven, which is remarkable when you think about today when most people can expect to reach eighty, almost twice what our grandparents might expect. As I write this, I am now into my eighty-second year. So statistically I'm on borrowed time and rather grateful to have that opportunity.

SHUT UP, SUIT UP, SHOW UP

From time to time, I've been asked to write about old age and dying, and with one exception, I always decline because, frankly, I find the subject boring, really boring. However, I do consider that a full embrace of aging and dying paradoxically is what gives us a maturity of experience and a richness of life. Flight from these matters of our ineluctable aging and mortality, which our culture helps us avoid, requires an avoidance of our essential appointment with destiny. Perhaps this sounds cynical, but what I have wondered when asked so often about writing about old age is, are people somehow expecting me or someone to make life easier, to make aging and dying ephemeral, to finesse it into something soothing and pleasant? Don't we all have an appointment with pain and loss and death to be kept? If so, I don't think this hidden hope is particularly conscious or intentional.

So why write about aging? Why not just face it, accept it, reflect on it daily so that your choices begin to matter to you, and get on with living in the best way you can, whatever the difficulties? So much that's been written and preached about aging strikes me as, to use a technical term, bullshit. Deep down we all know it. Sing a happy song. Look on the bright side and be sure to take all your vitamins today. All of that's well meant, no doubt, but bullshit really. So what I have to say about aging is simply three very simple points.

First of all, when you're really old, everything hurts—everything. So just deal with it. Second, the energy you once could count on to show up and support you is dicey, uncertain, and sometimes not there for the things you want to do. Third, an increasing number of the people whom you most love are gone and are never going to return. If none of those three conditions apply, then perhaps you are the one who is gone, the one whom they are missing.

Perhaps you can see why there are rather few requests for me to write about aging these days. Still, wherever there is learning to occur, an imagination to wonder, we're still alive, still growing, still in service to the mystery, regardless of the circumstances. I live in a four-story condo building in Washington, DC, and each day I take the elevator down to the garage to get to my car to go to work. On the elevator, when I'm usually there by myself, I say to myself, six words: "Shut up, suit up, show up."

I'll explain what I mean by that. First, shut up: You don't have any real problems. There are many people on this planet—and not very far from where you're standing at this moment—who have no home tonight, who have no food, whose children are being murdered. You don't have any real problems, so just shut up.

Second, suit up: Deal with life as it is. Do your homework, prepare, work hard at what matters to you.

Third, show up. That's all we can ever do. It's what Woody Allen meant when he said 90 percent of life is showing up. Do the best you can; that's all you can do. All of us feel flawed and sometimes failures in life. But all you can do is show up again today and tomorrow, the best way you can. Not in service to ego comfort but in service to what really matters to you.

MORTAL BODIES, IMMORTAL SPIRITS

Recently I taught a course on the poet Rainer Maria Rilke, and we read his poem "Autumn Day." In it, Rilke observes that nature is going about its final ripening. It's gathering resources for the wine press of time and the final fullness. But then he asks these questions: And are we doing the same? Are we consciously living in the face of gathering storms, conscious of our appointments with time but squeezing whatever we can from our experiences? He concludes the poem with these very piercing images (and implied questions for us): If you have no home by now, you never will. If you are alone, you will always be alone. You will spend your life reading into the night, writing futile letters, and wandering the lanes as a leaf blown by the wind.

How are we to understand those stark and perhaps harsh-sounding words? I don't think Rilke is speaking literally about having no outer house as a domicile. I think he's suggesting rather that we also, like nature, have to prepare ourselves for the journey, this full journey. Do we continue to set up projections onto the world, expecting others to fix it for us, to take care of us? Or have we owned our own stuff, our unfinished business, and are working at it as best we can? Are we adrift psycho-spiritually without a grounding in something that really matters to us? If not (and this is a common condition), then we really haven't been paying attention; we haven't been preparing for what depth psychology and spiritual teachers have told us for millennia: that the end of the journey is just as real and just as important as the beginning, and all the confusion in between.

I have several clients who are between sixty-five and eighty-plus, and I've noticed some interesting phenomena. Those who best handle the aches and the losses of the older years are those who have lived the richest, most risk-taking lives. Those who have not are most often caught up in fear, regret, remorse, and a vague dread. It's not enough to say that they dread dying. Rather, they more profoundly dread not having lived more fully first.

Another phenomenon I've noticed is even more interesting. For those who pay attention, the psyche's agenda for growth is endless and not tied to our aging bodies. Many of their dreams review each person's journey, bringing different stages into view, different people associated with each stage, sometimes even different geographies together in the same dream. Why might our psyche do that? Invariably it brings up old associations and forgotten places, times, people.

I know that our psyche is a meaning-making, meaning-requiring organ. I suspect that the reason for this stirring of our histories is for more than addressing unfinished business (though it may also include that). I think this is how our psyche sorts and sifts and helps us begin to identify the threads that run through our narratives, perhaps helping us make more and more sense of whatever engines have been driving our lives.

In another poem, Rilke recalls images from his childhood and allows their widening circles to amplify and stir even a transpersonal awareness of our common condition. He employs a "metonymy," the children's game of ball, to conjure up those past hours and link us to the greater mystery in which they (and we) all swim. Metonymy is a figure of speech, a literary device, a trick, or gambit whereby we bring up something that, by way of association, links us to the larger experience, maybe the part that is inexplicable. For example, I was very close to my grandmother, and when I was a child, I remember her working on her rosebushes. When I reflected on her passing years later, the image that pushed itself to the front of my consciousness was the scratches on her hands from the thorns of the rosebushes. That was a metonymy, a point of entry, an aperture, into a large, rich, inexplicable experience of a personality for I knew that she cared for me and did what she could to support me.

During that time of reflection of her, I wrote a poem that concluded with the lines: "Roses and thorns, scratches, and first blood, in the first scratch of time." The roses and their thorns scratching her wrists opened the metaphor of blood, and not only blood as vulnerability but blood as our kinship together. We shared a common blood. It was the first scratch of time, the first encounter with the experience of loss and suffering in time. The point of metonymy is to provide an aperture through the particular, through the specific, into a much larger realm that is in many ways inexplicable.

So back to Rilke and a poem from his *Sonnets to Orpheus* series.[1] Here is my translation:

Oh, you few, you playmates of long ago,
amid the scattered gardens of the past,
how we circled, shyly approaching each other, communicating
without words.
Joy was our common ground,
but how joy fled before all the gathering forces in the anxious years
to follow.
Strange coaches clattered around us.
Houses loomed large and phantasmal, and no one knew our
names. What was real in all that? Nothing.
Only the balls, their glorious curves, not even the children

for, alas, sometimes one of them, oh ephemeral,
would step beneath the falling ball.

To me, that poem is so evocative of a time passed, irrecoverable in some way and yet still present to us, still there as a phantasmal presence.

He recalls what it was like to be a child approaching other children, approaching the world with a sense of mystery and awe and, at times, intimidation; and events happening around us, like the coaches clattering by and the large houses looming phantasmal. And no one really knew who we were. Remember the old Zen parable: "I'm looking for the face I had before the world was made." In other words, what is our real name, the name that lies beneath the name we were given as children? And what was real in all of that? he asks. Given that it's such a rich and yet, in some way, time-obscured range of images, his imaginative self chooses the ball that they played with. He says, "Only the balls, their glorious curves, not even the children / for, alas, sometimes one of them, oh ephemeral, / would step beneath the falling ball." What a wonderful evocation of the fact that all of us are on the playing grounds of mortality. All of us carry, in some way, immortal spirits and yet are housed in mortal bodies. As I turned to the thorns of the rosebushes, the game of ball is his point of entry, the aperture, into the mystery that was both play and fate and destiny meeting as one simultaneous reality.

BRINGING OUR STORIES INTO CONSCIOUS LIFE

When you reflect on those earliest days and the formative hours, what comes up for you? What about those playmates that you knew? Maybe the kid down the block whom you were afraid of? The one who was your best friend? Who were they? Where are they today? What were their lives and journeys about? They're still alive in our psyches, even though we may not have seen them in decades or even thought of them. Ask yourself, what images arise from those days for you? Again, those images serve as metonymics—a particular image capable of intimating a larger often unapproachable atmosphere.

I recall a swing in the backyard of my childhood home, and I used to swing on that incessantly, imagining that it was my airplane. It was my need for risk, my need for flight. Or I recall climbing on roofs or to the top of trees. Both were a need for transcendence of the ordinary, to have a larger perspective than possible on the ground. That swinging or climbing was a time when I was most by myself and most present to myself. Do you remember such moments when you were most present to yourself? Reflect on how hard it is to have that sense of presence today with the thousand distractions we have around us.

What persists for you from those days? What stories? We've been talking a lot about stories in these chapters. What fragmental narratives are you still carrying that, like splinters beneath the flesh, wish to work their way toward the surface? Again, as noted in the William Faulkner novel *Requiem for a Nun*: The past isn't dead. It's not even past. I've learned (and I'm not always happy about this), and I imagine you have too, that many of the generative energies within me—the complexes, the wounds, the avoidances—keep showing up when I think I've left them far behind. This shows me the staying power of some of those energy clusters and how, for good or ill, they operate autonomously.

Many times I've had patients come in and say, "I'm so upset with myself. I thought I was past this or that. I thought this was behind me. And yesterday it came rushing back to me, and I fell into the same old place, or I was drowning in that old emotion." They berate themselves by thinking, *Life is just a linear process, and I must get beyond this issue.* But it's not linear. It's more circular, maybe spiral. We circle back on these things over and over and over.

Jung frequently noted that we don't solve our history, but we can outgrow it once we are aware. There's a big difference there. Some problems are not solvable because they're part of the history we bring with us, but we can outgrow their dominating influence. And, yes, they're going to show up from time to time. Each time they do, they bring to our consciousness, *Yes, this is still with you, but you also have an enlarged consciousness and capacity to address it today in a way you couldn't at that point.* Maybe that spiral process moves one cycle higher then. Because nothing that we've ever experienced has wholly left us, we must ask the probative question: What do those shards of history make us do, even today? Or keep us from doing, even today?

If we wish to understand ourselves, even gain a greater measure of freedom, then we have to bring these stories into greater conscious life. How can we ever choose freely if we don't know all the players on our inner field? You may think, *Well, I got beyond all of that,* or *This sounds very regressive.* But remember the basic point is our psyche is timeless, and given whatever is triggered in this new moment, the psyche is forever doing its data research instantaneously: Where have we been here before? What do we know about that? What do our histories tell us to do or not to do? That material floods consciousness and remains our binding to the past.

As we sort through these shards of experience, the psyche keeps threading into our dream scenes from our impulsive choices and our repetitive behaviors. There's more than enough work here sorting through this mélange of images, this debris-strewn history, to keep us busy for the rest of our journeys.

Again, this is not at all in service to any nostalgia or a desire for an earlier time. It's essential to figuring out now what is continuing to create our history. If we don't attend this inquiry, if we don't consider those images that arise from the depths of our soul, we remain but unconscious, unwitting colluders in the insurgent shaping of our history.

It's particularly difficult at times when we reflect on the painful moments in our lives, where we did something really stupid or hurtful to ourselves or to others or times that we feel bound to with shame. No one who is conscious or thoughtful is free of these. But even then, the psyche is seeking to bring them to the surface, to allow us not to be defined by them. Ask yourself the question: *If I ignore something, does it go away? Does it not, in some way, make its subterranean appearance and affect my behaviors, my choices, how I feel about myself, the basis out of which I make my choices, the grounding on which I stand?* Better to bring it all into awareness, lest it continue to operate autonomously and unconsciously. Jung said our greatest sin—to use that old-fashioned word again—is choosing to remain unconscious. Consciousness is difficult and sometimes attended by significant conflict. At the same time, an unconscious life is even more of a danger to self and a danger to others.

AMENDS, REPARATIONS, AND UNFINISHED BUSINESS

These forensic investigations of our psychic gardens will also bring to our attention people and situations that may still be crying out for our amends, for our reparation—where doing so does not cause further harm. What unfinished business awaits each of us? What are the developmental tasks I have delayed this long? Where do I still need to grow up? Where are my fears still standing sentinel, blocking the door to a larger life?

As I found in workshops through the years in various cities, and certainly working with patients, these issues don't go away. There are still developmental tasks for each of us, still parts of us that are infantile, that flee responsibility and flee accountability, and that try to ignore the genuine conflict that competing values represent in our lives.

Jung noted that sometimes our most troubling issues rise out of conflicts of duty—commonly a duty to others and a duty to ourselves. We have to attend to those duties and to ask: What is the larger perspective in this conflict of opposites? Where do I still need to grow up? Growing up means being accountable and doing something about it—not just complaining. Where do the fears still exercise their vetoes over our lives? Down in our psychic basement is a whole field of archaic anxiety that is easily triggered. It's like an electric current, and when something triggers it, the whole system is activated, and it shuts us down. We may, for example, still have primal fears of confrontation with others. Yet unless we're willing to stand for something that matters to us, we're not creatures of value. We're not living out of any kind of integrity. We're not persons of worth as we wish to be.

We still have the fear of being on our own, fears of abandonment. I've had more than one person say to me, when they were in terrible relationships or terrible work situations, "I won't let go of this hand until there's another hand in the darkness for me." Or, "I won't leave this security until I have security somewhere else." I understand that. I don't judge that. But I also know what stuckness is, and I also know that there's a refusal to step into the awesomeness of one's own journey. In so doing, we live a diminished life, a smaller life.

One of the questions that can be very helpful to ask ourselves from time to time is, Does this choice, does this juncture in my life, does this relational situation, does this work situation, or is the path I'm on make me a larger person or make me a smaller person? I believe we know the answer to that question. We may not wish to know the answer, we may flee the answer, but we know the answer. As the French philosopher Jean-Paul Sartre pointed out, we can live in mauvais foi or bonne foi—bad faith or good faith—with our own souls. Something in us knows, always.

Years ago, I wrote a book about what matters most in living a more considered life. The theme that popped up for me first, and I touched on this in a previous chapter, is it matters that we not live a fear-driven, fear-governed life. Of course, we can't avoid fear. It's part of the human condition. It comes from being a sentient being in a world that is risky, even lethal. But to have our life governed by fear is quite another matter. It can only lead us to a diminished life, a life much smaller than our souls wish of us. Again, we walk in shoes too small for us, as Jung said. Stepping into a larger footprint always occurs through stepping into and through what we fear. Most of all, what we fear is being out there on our own. Yet how can we ever lay claim to the worth and value of *our* life, *our* journey, unless we've stepped out from the known world, the secure world, into that world of possibility?

Many of those fears are wired to the archaic times in the basement of our histories. Activating their circuitry has the capacity to just shut us down. The old fears—the fear of the disapproval of the other, fear of abandonment, fear of punishment—are all real and compelling fears for the child and still constitute a secret sovereignty in the lives of so many adults. Aging doesn't solve that. I remember as a child having the normal fears of childhood, thinking that parents and even the big kids acted as though they were cool and knew what was going on. I thought, *Well, they must take us aside at some point and explain all this to us, and we'll be able to understand how to cope and be beyond fear.* Of course, that was my ignorance and my naivete. What I couldn't have known is that those big people, the giants around me, were mostly living lives governed by fear. Most of them were unable to even have access to the kinds of insights and conversations, such as the ones we're having here, that bring these things to the surface and help us examine them.

However, if we examine these fears, and if we catastrophize consciously to the worst case, we find these fears seldom materialize. They are phantasmal spectral presences. If they were to happen, often the psychological enlargement of our lives as we move through the fear is well worth the price of admission. If you are a child and the supportive other is suddenly not there, you may very well perish. If you encounter the power of the other and anger it, you may very well suffer grievous punishment and harm, and many children have. That gets wired in, and years later, the story quickly catastrophizes and goes to the worst possible outcome.

Yet if we reflect upon it, we realize that avoidance of the old fears ignores the possibility that there is an adult on the scene who stands by readily available to take life on, who has understandings, ranges of choice not available to the child, and, most of all, depth of resilience that maturation brings. This adult who is our guide and protector is, of course, ourselves. When the stories are activated and the old circuitry triggered, it takes us back to those places of abandonment.

Remember the pop singer I mentioned earlier who tried to dismantle her public image as a kind of unconscious, impulsive, but really heroic effort to break out of the bubble of career success that held her captive and owned her soul. We realize the terror of a person being trapped like that. It's so easy for someone outside to disdain a person in that struggle, and yet the Self itself organized that impulse seeking to free the person.

There comes a place where consciousness has to deal with these things. One of the roles that consciousness can play is to help tilt the balance. If I know there are areas where I'm still blocked by childhood fears, by old stories, by lack of cultural permission, or by old religious or educational admonitions or guilts, my consciousness can deal with that. It can say, *You know, it's more important to be honest about this stuck place in me. It's more important to live this journey as authentically as I can and not be owned by that.* Consciousness can help tilt the balance and move us into change and risk, knowing that when we're doing the right thing, the resources of life are there to support us. Something in nature rises to support us.

THE REMAINING TASKS OF PERSONAL LIBERATION

Getting on with the business of old age invariably involves addressing the remaining tasks of personal liberation before our sand runs out. You have to ask yourself, *What are the tasks that still wait for me to show up in my life? Where is fear still blocking my life, no matter what age I am?*

Many years ago, I had a client who had been diagnosed with an aggressive and terminal cancer. She realized her life up to that point had been governed by fear. She'd lived a safe conventional life, so much so that she had grown estranged from people, including her own children. She realized one day, "What is it exactly I'm afraid of? Here I am, about to die, and I'm still afraid of everything." Believe it or not—trust me on this—she took up skydiving and martial arts in her last months. I was astounded. Most of us do not have to risk these literal acts to begin to grow larger than our fears. Because she threw off the shackles of fear, she was able to share that it was the best time of her life. She said to me, "I wish this had come to me in some other way earlier in my life. It would've made a huge difference. But this is the best thing that's ever happened to me." And I believe it. I think those last months of her life, before she passed away, were the best years of her life because she was not governed by fear. She wasn't absent fear; she just wasn't governed by fear. There's a big difference.

We also need to remember that we learned from so many people, perhaps people that we took for granted at the time and little noted how they were mentoring us. I've always revered my teachers because I knew, even as a child, they were building bridges for me into a larger world. If I was to enter that big world, I knew I needed all the help I could get. We have to ask ourselves, *What have I learned along this serpentine highway I call my life? What can I pass on to others?* In my life, I so appreciated teachers that I became one. It's been the one thread of continuity in my work life all these decades. So please consider what you have to share and be the sort of person whose presence resonates through the generations that follow when we are gone.

All of this brings us to the central question: How am I going to continue to grow at least inwardly even as my external world declines? In his later years, when ailing of body, W. B. Yeats wrote,

> An aged man is but a paltry thing,
> A tattered coat upon a stick, unless
> Soul clap its hands and sing, and louder sing
> For every tatter in its mortal dress.[2]

The "tatter in [our] mortal dress" is the decay of our bodies, of course. When Yeats wrote those words, he was in physical pain and sick at heart for the many disappointments of his life. Now no young person is allowed to write words like that. One could only say to such a person, "Wait a few decades. Experience what life brings you, and then we'll see." Such a pronouncement sounds like cynicism, even bitterness, but it's not. It's simple realism. We don't know what's headed our way.

Long ago, I used to puzzle at an old Greek saying that I found in so many different tragedies and ancient texts: "Best of all is not to have been born. Second best is to have died young." I remember thinking how gloomy and pessimistic that view of life is. Now like an old tortoise that has been covered with scars and lumbering on nonetheless, I understand those lines. Those of us who have been privileged to have more years to live have accumulated more losses as well as more joys. What Yeats is talking about there is really about the necessity of concomitant inner development as the outer world grows progressively more difficult to manage.

I want to return to Jung's observation: "The flight from life does not exempt us from the law of age and death. The neurotic who tries to wiggle out of the necessity of living wins nothing and only burdens himself with a constant foretaste of aging and dying, which must appear cruel on account of the total emptiness and meaninglessness of his life."[3] To unpack that a bit, we may spend our lives as psycho-spiritual fugitives running from the important tasks of life, but our body and our psyche are moving us through the stages of the journey regardless. A person who tries to slip-slide out of facing the tasks of life really achieves nothing and yet, in some way, is dying a thousand deaths every day, which, as Jung points out, is especially cruel because such a person's life is already empty and meaningless. It's one thing to be afraid and risk the journey; it's something else to be fugitives in our lives.

NOSTALGIA ROBS US OF THE PRESENT

During the last years of his life, Yeats described himself as a wild, wicked, passionate old man. Perhaps that spirit is best found in one of his last poems, "The Circus Animals' Desertion." In this poem, Yeats reviews his life and compares himself to a ringmaster of a circus, one who summoned many personae in his grand tour, many stunning animalia, many high-wire acts. But he now knows the show is closing. The aesthetic sleight of hand, which once offered the youth the means of escape, what he termed his ladder up and out of the muck and mire of life's frequent struggles, has disappeared. Then he considers from whence those early fugitive flights, the confusions, the mishegas of midlife conflict and collision, and those later images of acceptance and transcendence emerged. He says all of those images:

> Those masterful images because complete
> Grew in pure mind but out of what began?
> A mound of refuse or the sweepings of the street,
> Old kettles, old bottles, and a broken can,
> Old iron, old bones, old rags, that raving slut
> Who keeps the till. Now that my ladder's gone,
> I must lie down where all ladders start
> In the foul rag-and-bone shop of the heart.[4]

The "raving slut" he talks about who tends the till on all of us is time and death and desiccation, and she returns us all to elemental earth. But encased in our rags—flesh-and-bone cage—the heart beats on. We are left with our humanity; our yearning for love, for divinity, for release, yet finally returning always to the heart, which thumping its disquietude still opens us to life, to death, and to the great mystery of it all.

We are grateful for the markers our predecessors left behind and the dark wood we all enter, but each of us must find our personal way through, as some did theirs before us. Bluntly put, for every outer decline, failure of powers, and environmental constriction, something within each of us is challenged and summoned to grow. Amid the wreckage of history, the carnage of loss, and the growing catalog of grief, the soul is summoned always to grow. As Yeats said, "Soul clap its hands and sing, and louder sing / For every tatter in its mortal dress."

I believe, even more today than ever before, that the quality of our lives will be a direct function of the magnitude of the questions we keep asking— questions we are now obliged to pursue for ourselves. When we were young, we all wanted and expected answers. Along the way, we learned that even good answers for today will be outlived by tomorrow. The more we hang on to the old answers, the more we're constricted by them. That's the dirty little secret of nostalgia. It takes us back to a place that never really existed and robs us of an emergent present. But we do have to ask these questions on our own because there is so precious little in our culture that does not elevate and privilege the banal, the distracting, and the trivial, all of which are affronts and diminishments of the soul.

You have to find questions that matter to you, questions that open you to a further journey. Let me suggest a few of those questions for you. These are questions that I think about and reflect on, and I find that they keep evolving and new responses emerge. All of which again suggests a developmental process rather than a static stuckness. These are basic questions we've touched on in prior chapters: Who am I, really, apart from all that history, all those relationships, all those scripts and obligations? It's so easy to confuse the manifest presence of the outer life, our curriculum vitae, and think, *That's who I am. I am my résumé.* Ask yourself: *What remains unfinished in me? What is still seeking respect? What is still wishing to be addressed? What is still challenging me? What fires my imagination still?*

That leads us to the question: *What was left behind, that which still waits to be honored by me, still is asking for respect, still is asking me to pay attention?* Also ask this question: *What links me to the larger?* What is the larger? How do you understand your journey in a larger frame, whether it's nature, a sense of the divine, your relationships in depth, the work of your hands or your mind or your imagination?

THE RECOVERY OF PERSONAL AUTHORITY

Wherever you're still curious, wherever your imagination still can address the task of life, you're fully alive. There's still an agenda there. When we do that, we realize life is still rich, still challenging. Yes, it's sometimes still intimidating. Yet it's our life, our journey, and our honor to attend that. Remember that quotation from Rilke that I've mentioned so many times: "Our task is to be defeated by ever larger things."

Of course, our sanguinary sea surge of aging and mortality are all the more troubling and unmediated for those cultures that have lost their mythic connection to the gods, to the transcendent powers, and to those great redeeming rhythms of death and rebirth of which we are such a tiny but inextricable part.

While our ancestors may have longed for reunion in another world with their lost brethren or understood themselves an ineluctable part of a great cosmic cycle in which life and death are one, more and more moderns experience their life as fugitive egos, adrift, homeless, bereft, disconnected from anything large or abiding. For good or ill, the modernist and postmodern eras have shifted the locus of accountability from the shoulders of the tribe or the sacred institutions to the shoulders of the individual.

Along with that swerve of assignment is the central task of the second half of life—the recovery of personal authority. Personal authority is always difficult for us. For our ego states are flooded with messages and warnings, seductions, and, increasingly, distractions. Sorting and sifting, sorting and sifting, we begin to find those threads that resonate for us, those in our bones we know to be true.

Consider the principle of "resonance." If something's real, if something's important for you, it will resonate for you. If someone else says this is important, that this is what you should think, feel, believe, do, and it doesn't resonate, then, well, maybe it's true for them but it's not your truth. Resonance is not something that we create. Resonance is an autonomous response of our soul when we are in right relationship to it. Resonance, re-sonance, re-sounding—the tuning fork inside of us hums. When we feel a sense of resonance, we live those summonses, those challenges. If they're not lived, we're still enacting what Jung called the provisional life, a life that someday could be real but is just a received script at this point.

The Danish philosopher and theologian Soren Kierkegaard talked about a person who awakened one morning to discover, to his dismay, that his obituary was in the newspaper. He was shocked to realize he died because he hadn't known he was really here. Our life may be full of bluster and bravado and high sentence perhaps, but not fully or really here.

Only through finding, risking, and living those truths that speak to us can we come home at last to ourselves. This summons is not to narcissism; quite the contrary. It's the summons to the service of something larger than we are, something larger than our ego comforts and reliable defenses.

In the face of our progressive physical diminishment, what we have is our continuing companion faculties: our imagination and curiosity. As long as they're present, we're alive and growing and developing. I believe that process goes up to and through our last moments of awareness.

Meanwhile, might we occasionally manage to stop whining and kvetching? The Irish playwright George Bernard Shaw put it once, let us risk "being a force of nature instead of a feverish clod of ailments and grievances, complaining that the world will not devote itself to making us happy."[5] Remember my six-word motto that I say every morning: shut up, suit up, show up.

Maybe we're all asked to risk letting go of our fearful tenuous grip on life, whereby ironically we remain enslaved to the fear of death. There are many ways of dying, and death is only one of them. Let's embrace dying into our previous life and the fear that keeps us from the new, lest we die before we die. Or, as the poet Johann Wolfgang von Goethe put it in his poem "The Holy Longing,"

> Until you have learned that death is the price of growth,
> and one must die to grow,
> you are only a perturbed visitor to this dark earth.[6]

As I reflect on my journey, it's been full of heartache and loss, but I've also had experiences of being loved and of loving others, and the richness of learning and discovery and travel. I'm so grateful for all of this. I would like as my epitaph, metaphorically speaking, my summation of the journey, to recall that it is a journey with many arrivals, many departures, and many, many more questions along the way.

I think that spirit was best embodied by a short untitled poem by Rilke published way back in 1905. Here's my translation of it:

I live my life in widening rings,
out over the world of things.
I may not be able to bring it all to completion,
but I will continue to try.
I'm circling around God, around the ancient tower,
and I've been circling for a thousand years.
And I still do not know if I'm a falcon, a storm, or a great song.

That poem, to me, speaks to the embodiment of the mystery that is found in each of us. How dare we run from the magnitude of the discovery that life asks each of us to address. The doing of which makes this life at times almost unbearably rich.

The summons to aging is the summons to reflect on what matters to us. We have tried and found things that don't work for us, things that do work for us, things that no longer matter, things we've outgrown, things that still matter to us. Living these verities is something we can risk these days. All of this revisioning of our journey is a summons to a humble accountability: What have the gods asked of me, what does life ask of me, and how best can I respond to it? When we do that, and keep doing that, we are fully alive, whatever our age, whatever our condition.

8

Living More Fully in the Presence of Mortality

In the last chapter, we addressed issues of aging, reviewed our journey, and began figuring out our unfinished business, what needs reparation, and what is still calling for us to grow and develop and shape up in some way. In this chapter, we'll take that a step further and look at how we can live more fully in the presence of mortality.

THE PROBLEM IS THAT WE ARE MORTAL AND KNOW IT

We have a problem here: we're mortal and very, very much aware of that fact. There are several ways this shows up in our lives. First is by making us conscious. There comes a point in your life development where suddenly you realize that the statistics you have seen or those articles you've read might conceivably apply to you as well. Mortality actually becomes real. One of the characteristics of the turn into the second half of life is our mortality is no longer an abstraction or something out there over the edge of the horizon but something real and personal to us.

That becoming consciousness was reflected in the words of the eighteenth-century sage Samuel Johnson, who once said nothing quickens one's attention sooner than the threat of the noose. There's always a part of us that wishes to live in denial and perhaps continue a life of distraction. I've always loved the poem "Fern Hill" by Dylan Thomas. If you don't know it, please give yourself the gift of looking it up and reading it. It's a portrait of his childhood days, his holidays, or his summer vacations at his aunt's apple farm in Wales.

But it's not really a poem about childhood; it's a poem about having *been* a child. Though he portrays the innocence of childhood, it's not a poem about innocence; it's a poem about having been innocent. The poem concludes with the reflection that, despite the giddy, carefree childhood, one day he would be ineluctably drawn to an awakening to mortality and limitation. None of that, however, would obviate his charged memory of having once been in the child's paradise of innocence, spontaneity, and wonder.

Of course, the awareness of mortality can also bring existential terror. Yeats wrote, "Consume my heart away; sick with desire / And fastened to a dying animal."[1] Notice he's aware his heart wishes to be immortal, and yet it's tied to a dying animal. What a metaphor. To consume the heart away would be to lose all feeling about it. Sometimes our awareness of mortality even brings us to humor. Many jokes toy with the idea of death and, in their own way, show that humans can find the freedom of laugh en route to the grave.

I can't help but reflect on the contemporary wisdom of one of our contemporary sages Paris Hilton, who said, "My biggest fear is to die because I have no idea what happens after. And I'm really scared that it's nothing because that would be beyond boring."[2] Well, you might want to spend a little bit of time, but not very much time, reflecting on the wisdom of that.

Let's look for a moment at how humankind has historically experienced our mortal condition. Aging, dying, mortality was less of a threat to cultures with a strong belief in an afterlife—belief that has diminished tremendously over the last two hundred years and particularly in the last fifty years in Western civilization. Same is true of cultures that participated in the second of the two great mythic journeys. One mythic archetype is "the quest," the developmental agenda; and the other is "the eternal round, the great circle," sometimes called the "saga of the Great Mother"—mythologies that emphasized death, rebirth, and the cycle of seasons. We slay nature in order to live, eating plants or animals, and nature ultimately consumes us as well. It's part of a great cycle, based on less ego identification and more of being subsumed into the reality of the wisdom of nature. But mortality, aging, and dying is the greatest affront to the fantasy of ego sovereignty. If ever we think we're really something, then we have to remember the democracy of the grave. You think of that famous poem "Ozymandias" by Percy Bysshe Shelley. He writes about coming across this ancient visage, half-covered with sand, and underneath that had been this proclamation by the pharaoh, who had put it up to boast of his achievements: "Look on my works, ye Mighty, and despair!" Shelley ends the poem by saying, "The lone and level sands stretch far away."[3] So much for sovereigns.

But really, the question of mortality confronts us every day with two other questions. First, what does my mortality make me do, or what does it keep me from doing? And second, how do I live more fully in the face of mortality?

The basic theory is that an aroused awareness of mortality is not the same as the fear of mortality. It's really a summons to be accountable and to see in what way our psychology responds to our mortality. It's not as if we have a choice.

THE MODERN WORLD'S TREATMENT PLANS FOR DEATH

There's a heroic ego ideal of the Western world. All the changes we've made in environmental control of water, heat and cold, disease, and lifestyle. Nutrition and modern medicine have brought us further comforts and extended life but not perpetuated it. More frequent longevity offers us the seductive intimation of perpetuation. I mentioned before, in the classical era, average life expectancy was midtwenties, and forty-seven in 1900. Now we say sixty is the new fifty, and seventy is the new sixty and so forth. As I mentioned in the prior chapter, the average length of life in the United States and United Kingdom at this writing is seventy-eight: seventy-six for men and eighty-one for women.

The obsession with the extension of this life most arises out of the diminishment of religious assurances. Earlier I cited Matthew Arnold's "Dover Beach," where he asks the question: If we can't have the assurances—which is increasingly true for most moderns—of an afterlife, and of course that would be another life and not this one, what is there to build one's life on? Notice how seldom the ego really asks the questions: Why, other than my nervous agenda, should I live longer? *Why* should I live longer? In service to what? Should I live longer than my children? Should I live longer than you? And why, other than, again, the ego's desire for its perpetuation? Meanwhile, we pollute and overpopulate the planet and speed toward its becoming a desolate and hostile home.

I've always been moved and touched by how Sigmund Freud faced his death in London in 1939 after many painful throat operations for cancer. Freud observed that his death would be of minimal consequence because he had already contributed his small piece of the human puzzle. He had nothing further to say. I'm moved by his calm, his courage, his finality, and most of all perhaps his lack of inflation of the ego, at least on that occasion. He brought his chip to the great mosaic life, and he did that to the best of his ability. What if we, like the Greek Tithonus, had earthly mortality? We could live forever. Could we really bear the loss of all those dear to us? The diminishment of the world we cherish? The meaninglessness of unlimited choice? Nothing would be meaningful because you do this for a century, and then you do something else for another century. With no mortal frame, nothing matters in the end.

It's precisely our mortality, paradoxically, that makes possible, even necessary, our need for meaning. Jung pointed out that the smallest of things with meaning is always larger than the largest of things without meaning. But our world, the modern world, has essentially evolved five treatment plans for this.

The first is frenzied activity. Keep busy, keep busy. That way this issue doesn't trouble your soul at all. As the American baseball player Satchel Paige once said, "Don't look back. Something might be gaining on you."[4] Second, we've developed a culture of numbing. Drugs and alcohol numb these sharp-edged questions. Third, as I pointed out earlier, is our culture of distraction. Remember Pascal's *divertissement*, the invention of the Jester to keep people from reflecting on the depth, dignity, and limits of their journey. Most of all, we've evolved into an obsession with aging, mortality, life extension—the fourth plan. We talk about heroic medical measures against the enemy or against nature. (Possibly the simplest definition of neurosis is when we're allied against nature. So maybe when we're most neurotic is when we are most in denial—in some kind of flight from nature naturing.) Fifth, there may be a splendid recovery of a pagan celebration of life here—the whole idea of *carpe diem*. Since we're here a short time, let's live it as fully as we can and fling ourselves into it.

On the other hand, I think this awareness of our limited journey can bring up a daily agenda for us. It's not morbid to reflect on this subject. That we think it might be morbid is really the complex speaking, isn't it? That's the nervous ego growing agitated again. Rather, it's a summons on a daily basis to address the task of wisdom. We're drowning in information, but information doesn't equal knowledge, and knowledge per se doesn't equal wisdom. How do I assemble knowledge amid the onslaught of information we have? How do I find the knowledge needed to help instrumentalize my life? In the end, what is it that matters? What is it that really is worth my commitment? Such an inquiry is furthered by our mortality.

THE ESSENTIAL ABSURDITY OF THE HUMAN CONDITION

A number of years ago when I was in Houston, the local archaeological society was celebrating its fiftieth anniversary. They decided to have a joint reading of the old Sumerian *Gilgamesh*. I was impressed at what they were doing. They had local celebrities, like the mayor, other city council people, and TV personalities, reading this ancient epic in a serial form. It took several hours to get through it, and they asked me to talk a little bit about the story, the myth of Gilgamesh, and what significance it might have.

When I reread it at this later stage of my journey, I was impressed with its wisdom and how closely it paralleled the struggle of the book of Ecclesiastes, which was ascribed to Solomon but is thought to have come from some unknown person of that epoch reflecting on the human condition. Both of these works look at the essential absurdity of the human condition—the recognition that we're born, live a short time, are fully aware of that, and are fraught at all times by this existential limitation.

Gilgamesh came from ancient Sumeria—which today is Kirkuk in modern Iraq—approximately 3,500 years ago. Ecclesiastes, out of the Jewish tradition by an unknown speaker, was written approximately 2,700 years ago. They are several centuries apart but reach the same conclusions; each one recognizes and is predicated on the essential absurdity of the journey.

The first line of the book of Ecclesiastes says, "I've tried all things and found it all equals hebel"—*hebel* being Hebrew for "mist." It's like mist in the hand. Grab it. And what is it? But each of them came out with the same three conclusions and recognitions. So, how are we to live in an absurd universe? First, address the present task that life has brought you. As Ecclesiastes says, "Whatsoever thy hand findeth to do, do it with thy might" (9:10). Throw yourself into it. Suit up, as I said. Prepare, do your homework, do what's needed. Address it with your full gift of energy.

Second, love those whom the gods have placed at your side. They are our precious companions on this journey.

Third, respect. Remember always respect. Remember the gods, remember that we're all part of some larger mystery. That's not bad advice after all these years, when we think about it. Throw yourself into the tasks life brings you, be grateful for loved ones and companions at your side, and remember the mystery.

A number of years ago, I was moved by the book *Freud's Requiem: Mourning, Memory, and the Invisible History of a Summer Walk* (which sadly is out of print now) by Matthew von Unwerth. Unwerth recounts a time in 1913, when Freud, Rilke, and their companion Lou Andreas-Salomé took a walk across a beautiful park in Vienna in the spring. All the flowers were out in their full glory, and when they reached the end of their walk, Freud turned and saw that Rilke and Lou Andreas-Salomé were morose, in a depressed mood state.

He asked them what the problem was. They said they were just overwhelmed by the beauty and by the transience of that beauty, how short-lived it was. Of course, as Freud pointed out, it's precisely its transience that makes it beautiful. If they were here every day in that way, you'd walk by them and never, never see them. It's because they're here a precious moment that that moment becomes precious.

Freud went on to write, in 1915, "Transience," what is probably his shortest paper. In there, he makes the point: It's precisely our transience that raises the question of meaning, that makes this life matter. If we were the gods, we would simply live one century into the next. Time and choice would mean nothing.

DENIAL, DISTRACTION, DEFLECTION

Let's turn now to the question of mortality and how we live more fully in its presence. I think that pathway will be found in looking at our psychologies. Because in the end, the issue of mortality really comes down to the ego and its attitudes. To make an obvious point, death is not a problem for nature. Death is not a problem for divinity, but it is a problem for ego consciousness and its attitudes.

Remember, we need an ego consciousness for the tasks of daily life. But the problem arises from the attitude of ego. Sensing its vulnerability, it arrogates huge powers to itself, and that's that old inflation that we talked about previously—hubris. The chief task of the ego is to protect the organism. Be sure to look both ways when you cross the street. But when it gets into twisting and stunting behaviors to pursue that end, it winds up being the chief source of the problem. The ego develops various defenses—for example, denial. Possibly the most pathological approach to our problems is denial. That reminds me, many years ago, the New Jersey Dental Association had some billboards around the state that said quickly, "Ignore your teeth, and they'll go away." Denial is pathological because these things don't go away.

A primary example of denial, I think, is the example of Jeremy Bentham. Bentham and John Stuart Mill were noted social and economic philosophers. They developed together the philosophy of utilitarianism—the greatest good for the greatest number of people. Bentham passed away in 1832 (same year as Goethe). He left behind a will that included a significant stipend for the University College of London and indicated that each year at some notable occasion, they would host a dinner in his honor and the guest of honor, at least a participant at the table, would be his embalmed sameness. You heard that right. His embalmed presence was to be rolled out to that table. This went on for many years. It was only a few years ago that they stopped this custom.

I've often wondered if one was a guest at that dinner, what would be the topics of conversation? Would it be polite to observe that one's host was looking a bit peaked? That there were some flies buzzing around? I don't know what would be appropriate conversation there. I made a little pilgrimage when I was last in London. To this day, you can go there and see in a glass case the embalmed body of his sameness, Jeremy Bentham. A very smart man in his lifetime but perhaps having missed something essential in the process and basing so much on denial. As a matter of fact, there's a camera there that records you as an observer of Jeremy Bentham every six seconds. It's put out on the World Wide Web, and you could later perhaps see yourself there observing Jeremy Bentham. So our first line of defense and most pathological is denial.

Then we have, of course, distraction and deflection. I remember meeting a person once whose life was a frenzy of social engagements. I said simply, "You live a distracted life." That one phrase suddenly made a whole assemblage of defenses collapse. She then examined her life of feeling undervalued, unworthy, and how important it was to live a life compensating for that. So we live in a life of distraction and deflection.

We have numbing of various kinds—from working constantly to drugs and alcohol—or we project our psychopathology onto others, or even to the Imago Dei (Image of God). There are what I would call, and I mean this respectfully, unhealthy theologies. Frankly Freud had a lot to say about that when he talked about how much of religious proclamation is the projection of parental complexes and a subtle manipulation of the horror and ambiguity of life, as well as the finessing of the mystery into terms acceptable to the ego. That kind of theology, in the long run, deals in bad faith—mauvais foi—with the mystery of mortality.

Yet is it too much to imagine that when the guy with a scythe shows up at our door, ego consciousness is be able to say, *Well, you weren't unexpected. So it's my turn now, and I've had longer and greater privileges than so many of my kind.* I don't think it's morbid for me to think about that. I hope that when that time comes, which could be any day, that I'm able to have that attitude. It's my turn. I've had longer and greater privileges than so many people I know and care about.

THE EGO'S FANTASY OF SOVEREIGNTY

The very fact that you and I are reflecting on this possibility makes it much more likely for an enlarged ego consciousness to contain and not be defined by the fears and defenses of that earlier immature, imperiled ego. When we look to classical Eastern thought, we realize how it's dealt with this in such different ways and maybe better ways than ours. The central work of Buddhism was the relinquishment of the ego's fantasy of sovereignty. Remember that Gautama, when he went into the world and was shocked by all the realities he ran into, concluded the great noble truths: First, that life is suffering, conflict, and mortality. Second, he noted and very psychologically astutely, the cause of that suffering is ego attitudes, not nature. Third, the solution is in the ego's capacity to relinquish its agenda in service to nature. That reminds me of the German word for "serenity," *gelassenheit*, which means essentially the condition of having let be or let go. Then he goes on to describe the eightfold path of how to live in this contingent world. When I look at classical Buddhism, I don't see him founding a religion or an institution. I see him essentially promoting a life based on a psychological principle of the basic humility of the ego in the face of what it can do and what it can't do.

In the Hindu tradition, this material life is just part of a gigantic recycling process in which we see that the investment of nature is not to our satisfaction but into rapid recycling. Our task is to free up the burden of karma, which is acquired from previous generations, to free subsequent incarnations, ultimately to a life of nirvana, or release into bliss.

We may also reflect on the wisdom of the serenity prayer written by Reinhold Niebuhr—the willingness and capacity to discern between what one can do and what one can't do. I've often thought what is so impressive about the 12-step approach is the beginning. The first step, after working so hard to find a "treatment" plan, is your worst nightmare: You're not in control, and your techniques are not working. They're making it more and more difficult, and they are digging the hole deeper.

When you stop and reflect on the stratagems that our culture has evolved, we realize essentially how ineffective they are and how they leave us in some way in a diminished position—in an addictive position and a position of ultimate frustration. Whatever our philosophies, our theologies, or our invasions, we're all in this process and are going to have to face it alone. Just as no one can live your life for you, no one can die your death for you. As the novelist E. M. Forster pointed out, that the two persons, the infant and the corpse, about from whence and whither to on this matter are notoriously silent on the issue. So, we have to figure these things out for ourselves in that short pause we call our life.

Not surprisingly, I suspect some of the wisest things ever observed about life and about death can be found in the work of Jung. In his beautiful essay "The Soul and Death," he writes,

> People who feared life when they were young, suffer later just as much from the fear of death. When they were young, one says they have infantile resistances against the normal demands of life. One should really say the same thing when they are old, for they're likewise afraid of life's normal demands. And we are so convinced that death is simply the end of a process that it doesn't occur to us to conceive of death as a goal and a fulfillment as we do without hesitation, the aims and purposes of your life in its ascendance.[5]

There's a lot to think about there. What I've observed as a therapist is those who've not risked living are the ones most fearful, most timid, most fugitive.

In Leo Tolstoy's 1885 novel *The Death of Ivan Ilyich*, Ivan Ilyich was wholly a creature of his time and place. He had had no thoughts about his own soul. He was simply a creature of adaptation. He pursued the right profession, married the right person, lived in the right neighborhood, espoused the right social and political attitudes, and everything moved smoothly along until one day there was a pain inside that wouldn't go away.

To make a long story short, he realizes that no one can help him with internal discord, and Tolstoy cycles the reader through the five stages of approaching acceptance (which the psychiatrist Elisabeth Kübler-Ross would outline so tellingly in the next century). He starts out first in complete denial and then moves to anger that his conventional life has been overthrown and upset. He then gets into bargaining one way or the other. Then he falls into despair. Then he ultimately comes to acceptance.

Obviously Tolstoy had observed this in the life and the dying of people all around him. Ivan represents a person who came to live only in his last three days of his life. He realizes no one was prepared to talk with him about it because it was someone else's problem, someone else's life, someone else's death, except a peasant, an illiterate peasant with whom he spent his last days, asking questions: What about my life, has it been wrong? How is it to be lived? He realized for the first time he is a living human being with a soul. And then he dies.

His wife wants to get estate matters settled as quickly as possible and move on. His colleagues want to know who can move into his slot at work. Several of the people at the funeral have a card game, and they want to get the funeral over so they can get back to their poker game. In other words, none of it matters. None of it is applicable because it was about Ivan and not about "me." Well, the fact that Tolstoy could write that novella is certainly illustrative of the fact that this attitude of the ego, of the irrelevance of mortality until it's mine, is rather commonplace. But again, those who live their best shots, who've taken the risks, are far more able to accept their passage. What I found is that they usually focus less on themselves and more on those whom they leave behind. (As I approach my mortality, my chief desire is to remain here with my wife and be of help to her, as she has been to me. And second, I am still so curious, so much still to learn.)

Perhaps our brother Socrates had one of the best perspectives. He reportedly said three things. Obviously, the first had to do with cleaning up unfinished business. "I owe a chicken to Asclepius—see that that's paid off." So he's addressing the debts that have accrued, the unfinished business, the amends that must be made. It's also true because Asclepius was the god of healing. Maybe he was seeing that in death there is a kind of healing that occurs. Second, he goes on to say, about death, "If there's an afterlife, then I'll have a chance to converse with the great philosophers; I look forward to it." Third, he says, "Or, if it's annihilation, then I can have a long sleep and by golly, I need the rest." Perhaps some of his attitude is applicable to us.

THE CONCEPT OF AN AFTERLIFE

Whatever we think, feel, project, and hope is but a construct, a limited ego purview. Whatever is true about mortality, the ego in dying is radically transformed— either annihilated or changed into something that we can't imagine. Reportedly, two famous Brits, one of whom was American and one Irish, Henry James and Oscar Wilde, had revelations at the end. Henry James said, as he felt his death imminent, "Ah, the Distinguished Thing." And "Distinguished Thing" probably was capitalized. It's a very Jamesian thing to do, going out with a sense of literary style. Of course, Oscar Wilde looked about on his death bed and said, "Either that wallpaper has to go or I do."

As I mentioned in the discussion on aging, there are many deaths besides death. Life is a series of attachments and losses, and we go on. As Yeats wrote, "Man is in love, and loves what vanishes."[6] Jung added, "From the middle of life onward, only those who remain vitally alive are those ready to die with life."[7] In all of these comments, I have no quarrel with the concept of an afterlife. I personally hope there is one because there are many people I want to see. I want to see my son. I want to see my brother. I want to see my parents and many more. I'd also like to meet Lou Gehrig and Abraham Lincoln at the same time. But in any case, that would be *another* life and not this one.

I do know we gain most from this life by living with the mystery, not trying to tack it down. Any understanding, any paradigm that we have will be over-thrown as our instruments and our questions get better. The meaning of our life, of this life, is not found in surviving. We don't survive. It's found in the way we lived this life. As the old liturgy has it, "Always in the midst of life we're in death." Two examples come to mind: A forty-year-old woman whose rela-tive comes to her and says very sweetly, "It's time to die." That was how psyche announced it was time to move on. The world she had known had played out, was over, finished, kaput; and a new life was beginning. I also told you the story of the woman who took up skydiving near the end of her life, who was driven by fear and lived a fugitive life until she suddenly realized, *What do I have to fear?* I never forgot her reply that she wished it had come to her earlier in a different form, but that it was the best thing that ever happened to her, because she realized that she was no longer bound by her fears.

My clinical experience of the overtly dying—I'm talking about those who understand they're in a very terminal phase of this journey—is suggested by Jung, in his essay "The Soul and Death." He said, "I was astonished to see how little to do the unconscious psyche makes of death. It would seem as though death were something relatively unimportant, or perhaps our psyche does not bother about what happens to the individual, but it does seem that the unconscious is at all times interested in how one lives and how one dies, that is to say whether the attitude of consciousness is adjusted to dying or not."[8]

Notice the profundity of Jung's observation. What he observed in the overtly dying is that the unconscious is not really responding the way the ego responds. It seemingly is closer to nature and the will of nature than the ego, which is an artifact of civilization that's based on top of and often at the denial of nature. But the unconscious, as he says, it is not concerned about death. It's whether we're living in the meantime, and whether we're in some way in proper relationship to our death. In the end, as in most areas of life, it little matters what we think. It does matter what nature or divinity thinks. Our task is to align ourselves as much as possible with the movement of that other. This aligned harmony may be what is meant by wisdom.

Physical death is only one form of dying. There are other forms of dying. We die whenever fear governs our choices. We die when we sacrifice growth for security. Remember ego consciousness is interested in security at all costs, predictability, and as much control as possible. When that prevails, we live in fortresses. We live in stuck places. We're not growing and developing. We die when we sacrifice growth for security. Growth always will lead us into the unknown, which means some loss of security. We die whenever we choose a convenient certainty over an inconvenient mystery. Certainties are the ways in which the ego comforts itself, deals with the anxieties that rise out of lack of clarity, ambivalence, ambiguity.

The human ego really doesn't like ambiguity. We want clarity, predictability. Yet life is much more complex than that. The only way to truly respect it is to realize it's a mystery. It continues to unfold. What we think and feel today may be functional, or maybe not, but it will in any case prove inadequate tomorrow. When we live with that process and grow into it, then we are in right relationship to the essential mystery.

Jung observed that deviation from the truths of the blood begets for all of us a kind of neurotic restlessness. Restlessness suggests a disconnect from meaning.

The lack of meaning in life is the sickness of the soul, he said. You may recall the old saying from the theater, "Death is easy, but comedy is hard." It's easy to have a death scene on the stage, but it's hard to pull off humor. When we think about it, we realize death is actually easy. Nature takes care of that for us. You don't have to worry about that. Life is what's hard. The meaning of our life is found precisely in how luminously we live this brief pause between two great mysteries. Before finding out where we may or may not be going, it might be more productive to be sure first that we manage to be here in the first place.

FINDING OUR ARCHETYPAL RESOURCES WITHIN

As we reflect on this question of mortality, I'm sure a lot will depend on the stage of your journey, your chronological age, maybe your psychological age, but it is useful to remember that this is a natural process unfolding, to align ourselves with that process, and to ask appropriate questions along the way: What are the attitudes we need? What are the practices we need to stay fully alive? I will touch on several of these.

We began with where we set out, looking at how we got the formative stories of our life and recognizing the necessity of understanding their meaning. We're the creature that desperately needs and wants to have this mean something, so we try to provide stories about what happened: What was that about? What did it say about you? What did it say about me?

We recognize that whatever the stories we experience—whether generated by us in a reflective effort to make sense of life; by our reading of our environment; imposed upon us by institutions; by the time and place in which we live; or from social, economic, or other forces—are inimical to the natural unfolding of the individuation process. We can often paper over that division, that abyss that begins to grow within us, but there comes a time when we're not able to paper over it anymore. Our signals of distress from the unconscious will grow apace. It's the psyche's way of reaching up, tapping us on the shoulder, and grabbing hold of us.

As I mentioned, at midlife, when having achieved outwardly all the things that I thought were important for me to achieve, the psyche reached up and pulled me under into a world of depression. My first hour of therapy was not approached as the beginning of the second half of life. It felt like a miserable, confusing defeat of something about which I knew very little. It was just the beginning of a lifelong process, but it got my attention and made all the change in the world.

When we begin to explore our journey, ourselves, our psychology, the choices we made, and why we made those choices and not other choices, we realize that there are whole areas that are walled off from the sphere of consciousness.

They're pushed into the shadow world, not just to the unconscious but to the shadow. Remember the shadow contains those parts of ourselves or of our groups that when we make them conscious are contradictory to our values, threatening to them, or perhaps pose challenges for us that are intimidating.

Part of how we begin to move to a greater and greater awareness of the richness of our journey is through the exploration of our shadow. People who want to split off the shadow and ignore it all together either have it spilling into the world through their unconscious behaviors or are projecting it on to other people and seeing the fault in others. The more they disown their inner life, the more they're actually experiencing a life of self-estrangement.

Then we realize that we all have certain universal tendencies, certain universal needs, certain universal assumptions, and false choices. Those false choices are what our ancestors called "sin," which is the inability to always be dead-on target as to where life wants us to focus. Whatever is not addressed within us psychologically will show up in our patterns of greed, gluttony, anger, or destructive behaviors. Things never go away. They go somewhere else.

In addition, we are living in haunted houses. There are all kinds of invisible presences—presences that intimidate us, presences that remind us of something, presences that urge us to do something else or block us. Recognizing those invisible presences is the beginning of gaining a greater degree of psychological and spiritual freedom. We carry ancestral voices going back many years and many generations. We also carry the burden of the unconscious life that has been accumulated by those generations. We find ourselves, at times, living between the worlds—the world itself out there, changing ways of understanding, modes of belief and practice, what we assume to be received and stable values now challenged and deconstructed—or we find intrapsychically that our understanding of the world, our road map, is no longer applicable.

When that happens, we find ourselves adrift and in dismay. Each of us has to find that personal resilience, that sense of interior guidance that allows us to chart our pathway without which we will become subsumed either by psychopathology, such as depression, addiction, or self-medication, or caught up in the fevers and disorders of the world around us.

As we age, we realize each stage brings about a new agenda. Some of the old issues persist, but some drop away and some new ones come on board. Part of our task is to be aware of what this stage is asking: Where am I to deal with limitations, and where are my areas of growth? Where are my areas of challenge?

Lastly, all of this is a journey toward a revisioning of the ego world as we know it. The paradox is that anything that we think, feel, believe, or wish out of that limited purview is pure speculation. Such a transformation as mortality brings to us is beyond our powers of imagination. Death is either annihilation or transformation into something else. And I am rather certain we'll all find out. But one of the things we have to remember is there are resources within us that nature has given us, archetypal resources. We are not alone in this journey. Many have been on the journey before us. It is so heartening to be able to learn from the written records that people have left behind how they faced the terrible dragons, faced the fears, and somehow came through. Not everybody survived, not everybody got through, but some did. They did by willingness to risk things, to find courage.

Jung once wrote what this work requires of us. In my paraphrase, he said, "First, what we call psychology can only help with one of the three tasks. Psychology can give us insight, awareness of things, and that can be a very instrumental tool in conducting our journey." But he said, "Then comes the quality of character of that individual."

Second, he said, is courage. We can't give courage to another person. They have to find it within themselves. Sometimes that courage comes out of desperation, but it's there. Third, he said, is endurance, persistence, sticking it out. Insight, courage, and endurance. Out of that comes a change, out of that comes an enlarged life.

Jung, Rilke, and so many other sources from the ancient world and the modern world have pointed out to us that we are equipped with resources to live this journey. We are able to find in us places of support and insight. Remember this: something in us always knows what is right for us. There may be all kinds of obstacles between us as an ego consciousness and what is right for us. We may be intimidated by that. We may be lacking models in how that's done, but something is always telling us what is right for us.

Also, there is always a calling to accountability. All of the great religions and great philosophies of life have emphasized that no matter what happens, we're accountable for how this journey turns out. Yes, grievous harm can come to all of us. Large events outside of us shape and change the contour of our choices. At the same time, we are summoned to bring to the table our best psychological resources, our best psychological understandings, and our best understanding of psychological resilience. And with that, we find a way.

When we're doing what is right for us, something in us supports us. When we're doing what is wrong for us, there's something in us that opposes us. We all know that, but we've lost that central fact. We've lost that central understanding that the compass of which Emily Dickinson spoke is within each of us.

Conclusion

What Does the Psyche Want?

Many years ago, my dog had surgery. I said to the veterinarian as my dog was returned to my arms, "When do I let him get up and walk around?" He looked at me like I had three heads. He said, "Look, he's a dog. He knows. He'll tell you when it's right." I thought, *Oh, oh yeah, of course.* Of course, what the veterinarian was telling me, and why I've remembered this story, was a reminder that the dog lived with a vital relationship to his own guiding instinct. We are separate from our instincts and live by rules and prescriptions and schedules. The dog knew when it was time to get up and walk around because he was experiencing his own inherent healing process. And when it was time for him to go, he also knew that, and he withdrew from our companionship, withdrew to a place in himself to meet the end that fate brings to all of us. I've learned so much from that Lhasa apso named Shadrach.

We have that same instinct within us. We know what is right for us, and something in us is supporting us and directing us and guiding us. You won't know this until you've risked it yourself. You won't know this until you've finally made that exploration into the greater adventure.

I discussed active imagination in a prior chapter, and I wanted to mention just one more example. In a dream, I found myself in the former Führerbunker outside of Berchtesgaden in Germany, which I had in fact visited with my family. While it had been dynamited by American troops when they took over that area, the tunnel was still there, and we walked through it. In the dream, I was there, but I had lost my child, an eight-year-old at the time. Of course, as any parent would be, I was frantic. In the dream, I ran to the little village of Berchtesgaden, and I remember going to the police department, the fire department, the local religious establishment, the local school, and none of them could help me find my child. I was disconsolate, and I wandered back into the forest. Suddenly I saw a presence growing up out of the floor of the forest. It was a human shape, a large figure. He told me his name was Urgus, and he said, "I will help you find your child." I knew that he was telling me the truth and that I would need to pay attention to him.

Now, *ur* is the German preface for primal or archetypal, and *gus*, of course, we have gustatory, of the senses. (My grandfather, whom I never got to meet, was Gustav from Sweden). This imaginal figure represented the archetypal resources of a deep grounding in nature that had been cut off so much from my early life and probably disappeared at around eight years old in my adaptive journey. Yet here also, the same psyche that was assaulting my ego structure via the witch on the one hand was on the other hand providing a deep countersource of energy that arrived to help recover the lost child, to revivify that part of my psyche that had been shut down.

This was the beginning of many conversations I had with Urgus. He became a deeply valuable resource, a source I can still turn to because there's a place within whereby that psychic energy, once you have made friends with it, is yours for life. It becomes a constant companion for you.

I could cite many other dreams of people who've gone through perilous journeys or active imaginations where they have found, in their dialogue with the images that arise from the unconscious, something within them that's reaching out to them, something within them that is offering resources.

What I'm describing, from the standpoint of our culture, is the biggest pile of nonsense you've ever heard. It remains nonsense until you experience it yourself; until you explore your own psychic resources; until you realize the insights, the sources, and sometimes the frightening issues that are brought up. It's not always a pleasant journey. Until these things have become real for you, psychologically they're not going to be integrated into your life. They're not going to be part of how you live your journey. This psychological material represents the wisdom of nature, our nature.

Our ancestors knew it. They were connected to it. It gave them the guiding dreams. When Jung talked about how the individual gets separated from the sources of insight, he said that when a person is thrown into darkness they are also summoned to a journey in which a new light will emerge, and a supportive energy.

Unless you have found that in your own journey, it remains simply talk out there. But this is real. It's been reported through the centuries. It's the reality of the human psyche. It is a mystery. We know very little about it. But it is tangibly real. The word *psyche*, again, remember, is the Greek word for soul. It comes from two etymological sources. First is the verb *psychein*, "to breathe." It's that life force that moves through us; that inspiration, respiration, the breath of the invisible life energy that courses through the body and animates it, ensouls it.

Second, it was related to the image of the butterfly. Something that transforms from the pupae over time into something beautiful. It's elusive; you can't quite get your hand on it, but it flits away and yet is stunning to behold. These were the primal, metaphoric threads of the ancient imagination that sought to intimate the mystery of the psyche.

Our ancestors knew this, and there are many reports left behind. We are the beneficiaries of the reports left behind. The key, then: Can you risk this step into your own life, pay attention to the dreams, pay attention to the symptoms, ask what the psyche wants? We know what the world wants; we've been hearing that from our earliest days. We know what our parents want; we know what the employer wants; we know what popular culture wants. What does the psyche want? That's a whole different question. It's not narcissistic, inflationary. It's humbling. It will lead us to places that we may not want to go, but we're meant to be there.

Asking what the psyche wants means we may regain that internal compass that Emily Dickinson wrote about: If the sailor cannot see the north, she knew the compass can. We all have a compass, and the question is, do you know you have one? Do you know how to access it? Do you risk trusting it?

I hope these chapters have provided insights for you, support for you, and a reminder to you that we all have unfinished business to which to attend. When we attend to that unfinished business of the soul's journey, we become less of a problem to our culture and our society. We open greater vistas for our children and our neighbors. We find that in the end, our life journey is fascinating after all.

As I've said to many a client, this is not about curing you. You're not a disease. This is about making your life more interesting to you. It *is* an interesting journey, and it continues to unfold in challenging ways. The new mystery is as near as tonight's dream. I wish you well in exploring that unfolding mystery that wishes its expression in the world through each of us.

Notes

CHAPTER 2: WHEN THINGS FALL APART IN THE MIDLIFE TRANSIT

1. Dante Alighieri, *The Vision of Hell*, trans. Henry Francis Cary (Minneapolis: University of Minnesota, 1892), 3.
2. Encyclopedia.com, "Archaic Torso of Apollo," encyclopedia.com/arts /educational-magazines/archaic-torso-apollo#Criticism.
3. Rainer Maria Rilke, "The Man Watching," michaelppowers.com/wisdom /rilke.html.

CHAPTER 3: SHADOW ENCOUNTERS IN PERSONAL AND PUBLIC LIFE

1. Maxine Kumin, *Our Ground Time Here Will Be Brief* (New York: Penguin Books 1972).
2. Heinrich Heine, *Tragödien: nebst einem lyrischen intermezzo* [Tragedies along with a lyric interlude] (Berlin: Dümmler, 1823), 148, google.com /books/edition/Trag%C3%B6dien/cQR-hS9rW9sC?hl=en&gbpv=1.
3. Terence, *Heautontimorumenos*, 163, la.wikisource.org/wiki /Heautontimorumenos.
4. Carl Jung, *Psychology and Religion* (New Haven, CT: Yale University Press, 1960), 101.

CHAPTER 4: THE SEVEN DEADLY SINS THROUGH A PSYCHOLOGICAL LENS

1. Thomas V. DiBacco, "The Declarations of Coolidge," *Washington Post*, July 1, 1988, washingtonpost.com/archive/lifestyle/1988/07/01/the -declarations-of-coolidge/25dd8abf-79ea-459a-9846-36e45ac01f84/.
2. Louis Chevalier de Jaucourt, "Guttony," *The Encyclopedia of Diderot & d'Alembert Collaborative Translation Project*, trans. Sean Takats (Ann Arbor:

Michigan Publishing, University of Michigan Library, 2006), quod.lib
.umich.edu/d/did/did2222.0000.665/--gluttony?rgn=main;view=fulltext.

3. Walter Pater, *Studies in the History of the Renaissance* (London:
   Macmillian1873), 259.

4. Edna St. Vincent Millay, "First Fig," *Poetry* 12, no. 3 (June 1918).

5. Augustine, *Confessions*, gutenberg.org/files/3296/3296-h/3296-h.htm.

6. Rainer Maria Rilke, "The Solitary," *Das Buch der Bilder* [The book of
   images] (Berlin: Axel Juncker Verlag, 1906). Author's translation.

7. Rainer Maria Rilke, *Letters to a Young Poet*, trans. Stephen Mitchell (New
   York: Norton, 1993).

8. William Shakespeare, *Richard II*, act 3, scene 2 (London, 1597).

9. Homer, *The Odyssey of Homer*, trans. Richmond Lattimore (New York:
   Perennial Classics, 2007), 97, aub.edu.lb/fas/CVSP/Documents/Fall%20
   2017-2018/Fall%202017-2018/The%20Odyssey.pdf.

10. Fyodor Dostoevsky, *Notes from Underground*, trans. Constance Garnett
    (Project Gutenberg, 1996), gutenberg.org/cache/epub/600/pg600.txt.

CHAPTER 5: DISPELLING THE GHOSTS
WHO RUN OUR LIVES

1. Diane Wakoski, "The Photos," in *Emerald Ice: Selected Poems 1962–1987*
   (Santa Rosa, CA: Black Sparrow Press Press, 1988); see also Poetry
   Foundation, poetryfoundation.org/poems/46664/the-photos.

2. Carl Jung, "The Psychological Foundations of Belief in Spirits," in *The
   Structure and Dynamics of the Psyche* (Princeton, NJ: Princeton University
   Press, 1960), 309.

3. Adam Zagajewski, "Unwritten Elegy for Krakow's Jews," trans. Clare
   Cavanagh, *The New Republic*, April 6, 2011, newrepublic.com/article
   /86338/elegy-krakow-jews-poem.

4. Henrik Ibsen, *Ghosts and Other Plays*, trans. Peter Watts (New York:
   Penguin, 1964,) 61.

5. Philip Both, "Journey Out of a Dark Forest," *New York Times*, March 25,
   1962, archive.nytimes.com/www.nytimes.com/books/99/04/25/specials
   /frost-clearing.html.

6. Wakoski, "The Photos."

CHAPTER 6: FINDING PERSONAL RESILIENCE IN TIMES OF CHANGE

1. Matthew Arnold, "Stanzas from the Grande Chartreuse," 1852, cola.calpoly.edu/~pmarchba/TEXTS/POETRY/M_Arnold/1855 _StanzasfromtheGC.pdf.

2. Matthew Arnold, "Dover Beach," 1867, poetryfoundation.org/poems /43588/dover-beach.

3. W. B. Yeats, "Nineteen Hundred and Nineteen," *The Tower*, 1928.

4. C. G. Jung, *The Collected Works of Carl Jung*, vol. 13, trans. R. F. C. Hull (Princeton, NJ: Princeton University Press, 1967), para. 54, academia.edu /9234735/Carl_G_Jung_Vol_13_Alchemical_Studies.

5. Archibald MacLeish, "Hypocrite Auteur," *Collected Poems 1917–1982* (New York: Houghton Mifflin Harcourt, 1952).

6. Steven Levingston, "Like Vladimir and Estragon, We Wait for Our Godot. And We Wait," *Washington Post*, April 3, 2020, washingtonpost .com/outlook/like-vladimir-and-estragon-we-wait-for-our-godot-and-wait /2020/04/03/8249cd2c-745c-11ea-a9bd-9f8b593300d0_story.html.

7. Emily Dickinson, "Letters from Dickinson to Higginson," June 7, 1862, archive.emilydickinson.org/correspondence/higginson/l265.html.

8. Christopher Fry, *A Sleep of Prisoners* (New York: Dramatists Play Service, 1953), 61.

9. Rainer Maria Rilke, *Letters to a Young Poet*, trans. Stephen Mitchell (New York: Norton, 1993).

10. Marion Woodman (in-person lecture, Jung Center of Houston, Houston, Texas, in the late 1990s).

CHAPTER 7: REVIEWING THE JOURNEY

1. Rainer Maria Rilke, *Die Sonette an Orpheus* (Leipzig, Germany: Insel-Verlag, 1923), de.wikisource.org/wiki/Die_Sonette_an_Orpheus.

2. William Butler Yeats, "Sailing to Byzantium," public-domain-poetry.com /william-butler-yeats/sailing-to-byzantium-180.

3. Carl Jung, "The Soul and Death," in *The Structure and Dynamics of the Psyche* (Princeton, NJ: Princeton University Press, 1960), 405.

4. William Butler Yeats, "The Circus Animals' Desertion," poetryfoundation .org/poems/43299/the-circus-animals-desertion.

5. George Bernard Shaw, "Epistle Dedicatory to Arthur Bingham Walkley," *Man and Superman* (Cambridge, MA: University Press, 1903), bartleby .com/157/100.html.

6. Johann Wolfgang von Goethe, "Selige Sehnsucht," *West-Ostlichen Divan*, 1814. Author's translation.

CHAPTER 8: LIVING MORE FULLY IN THE PRESENCE OF MORTALITY

1. William Butler Yeats, "Sailing to Byzantium," public-domain-poetry.com /william-butler-yeats/sailing-to-byzantium-180.
2. Paris Hilton, in *The American Meme*, documentary film directed by Bert Marcus, 2018, subslikescript.com/movie/The_American_Meme-8106160.
3. Percy Bysshe Shelley, "Ozymandias," 1818, public-domain-poetry.com /percy-bysshe-shelley/ozymandias-31349.
4. M. B. Roberts, "Paige Never Looked Back," ESPN.com, espn.com /sportscentury/features/00016396.html.
5. Jung, "The Soul and Death," 405.
6. William Butler Yeats, "Nineteen Hundred and Nineteen," 1921, csun.edu/ ~hceng029/yeats/yeatspoems/NineteenNinete.
7. Jung, "The Soul and Death," 407.
8. Jung, "The Soul and Death," 407.

Bibliography

Dostoevsky, Fyodor. *Notes from Underground*. New York: Vintage, 1994.

Heraclitus, *Fragments*. New York: Penguin, 2003.

Hollis, James. *The Eden Project: In Search of the Magical Other*. Toronto: Inner City Books, 1998.

_____. *Finding Meaning in the Second Half of Life: How to Finally, Really Grow Up*. New York: Avery, 2006.

_____. *Hauntings: Dispelling the Ghosts that Run Our Lives*. Asheville, NC: Chiron Books, 2013.

_____. *What Matters Most: Living a More Considered Life*. New York: Avery, 2009.

Jung, Carl. *Psychology and Religion*. New Haven, CT: Yale University Press, 1938.

_____. "The Soul and Death," in *The Structure and Dynamics of the Psyche*. Princeton, NJ: Princeton University Press, 1978.

Rilke, Rainer Maria. *Letters to a Young Poet*. Translated by Stephen Mitchell. New York: Norton, 1993.

_____. *The Poetry of Rilke*. Translated and edited by Edward Snow. New York: North Point Press, 2009.

Shay, Jonathan. *Achilles in Vietnam: Combat Trauma and the Undoing of Character*. New York: Simon and Schuster, 1995.

Zorn, Fritz. *Mars*. New York: Knopf, 1982.

Index

abandonment, 7–9, 122

accountability, 15, 58, 108–9, 121, 129, 144

   shift to individual accountability, 127

   mortality, 133

Achilles, 67–68

active imagination 110–13, 145–46

addiction, 7, 63

afterlife, 140–43

   see also mortality

aging, 114–29

   fear, 122–23

   personal authority, 127–28

   personal liberation and taking risks,
      124–25

   questions to ask yourself, 126–27

   shut up, suit up, show up, 116

   see also mortality

analysis, 15–17

anger, 66–68

anxiety, 43–44, 66

Arnold, Matthew, 98, 133

avoidance, 7–9, 56–57, 66, 90

   see also fear

Augustine of Hippo, 62, 65, 73, 76

authority (personal authority), 58, 127–28

belonging, 37–38

Bentham, Jeremy, 137

berserk, 67

betrayal, 92–93

Camus, Albert, 104

character, 24–25, 54, 144

   see also accountability

childhood, 5–6, 8–11

choices, 2, 5, 11–12

codependency, 8

complexes, 8, 80, 83–86, 96, 101

   cultural complexes, 81–82, 94–95

   parent complexes, 83, 86–89

   power complex, 8–9

   see also ghosts/hauntings

compromising, 8–9

connection, 37–38, 64, 73

cosmic plan, 102–3

courage, 13, 16, 144

   see also accountability

Dante, 28, 64–65, 68–69, 72, 74

death, 20–21, 58, 69, 126–28, 133, 136,
   141–42

   "The Soul and Death" (Jung), 138–41

   see also mortality

The Death of Ivan Ilyich (Tolstoy), 139

defeated by ever larger things, 39–40

depression, 11, 23, 29, 93

desire, 62, 64–65

destiny, 24–31

   defeated by ever larger things, 39–40

   fate, 24–25

   tragedy, 24

Dickinson, Emily, 104–5
disassociation, 7
diversion, 107
divinity, 38, 87
    inspiration, 14
    God, 49, 62, 94, 98–101
    see also mystery; myths; numinous; soul
Dostoevsky, Fyodor, 44, 75, 98
"Dover Beach" (Arnold), 98
dreams, 2–3, 82, 111–13
    active imagination, 110–13, 145–46
    midlife-related, 19–20, 22–23, 26–28
    parent-focused, 26–28, 88–89
    writing down/journaling, 15

ego, 4, 12–13, 17, 20–21, 43, 48, 136
    death and dying, 141
    god/myth, 99–100
    hubris, 25, 68
    id, ego, superego, 52
    incorporating more complexity, 29–30
    personal authority, 127
    questioning/examining, 55
    sovereignty, 137–39
    vocation, 13
elderly. *See* aging
Eliot, George, 98
Eliot, T.S., 44
envy, 69–71
epicureanism, 64
evil, 30, 41–42

fate, 24–25
    see also destiny
fear, 30, 39, 54, 57, 80, 122–23
Freud, Sigmund, 7, 52, 135
    Civilization and Its Discontents, 52
    death of, 133

id, ego, superego, 52
    nacherzieung (reeducating), 31
    repression, 7
Fry, Christopher, 105

ghosts/hauntings, 78–79
    cultural hauntings, 94–95
    relational ghosts, 90
    see also complexes, presences
Gilgamesh, 134–35
god(s). *See* divinity; myths

gluttony, 62–64
grace, 68, 74–75
greed, 71–73
guilt, 43–45, 91–93

hamartia, 24–25, 61, 68
hauntings. *See* ghosts/hauntings
Hector, 67–69
hero/heroine, 74
home, 37
hubris, 24–25, 52, 68

Ibsen, Henrik, 81–82
imagination (active imagination), 110–13,
    145–46
inadequacy, 8
insight, courage, endurance, 144
inspiration, 14
instinct, 14, 97, 145
intrapsychic imago, 32, 80, 86

jealousy, 69–71
Jung, Carl, 1, 26, 38
    active imagination, 110
    hero/heroine, 74
    insight, courage, endurance, 144

instincts, 14, 16
Jung's family, 87, 104
Memories, Dreams, Reflections, 50, 87
mythic gods, 99
neurosis, 31
"The Psychological Foundations of Belief
   in Spirits," 79
Self, 16
"...shoes too small for us," 26, 122
"The Soul and Death," 138–41
Symbols of Transformation, 30
see also complexes; shadow concept

karma, 62, 95, 138
Kissinger, Henry, 86
Kumin, Maxine, 41–42

lethargy, 39, 74
loneliness, 38, 63, 65
love, 65–66, 80, 135
lust, 64–66

manifest destiny, 46
Mantel, Hilary, 13
middle passages, 23–24
   see also midlife crises
midlife crises, 19–23
   defeated by ever larger things, 39–40
   destiny, keeping our appointment with,
      24–31
   dreams (midlife-related), 19–20, 22–23,
      26–28
   idealism to realism, 32
   middle passages, 23–24
   numinous, encountering and tracking,
      34–40
   reconstructing map of self and world,
      31–34

mortality, 131–34
   afterlife, 140–43
   denial, distraction, deflection, 136–37
   see also aging
mystery, 35–36, 38, 102, 129
   see also numinous
myths, 94, 99, 102
   cosmic plan, 102–3
   Greek and Roman, 99–100: Achilles,
      67–68; Hector, 67–69; Odysseus, 74,
      106; Olympus, 94, 99–100; Pan, 97;
      Zeus, 99–100
   Gilgamesh, 134–35
   see also divinity; numinous

neediness, 9, 91
neurosis, 30–31, 97, 100, 134
Nietzsche, Friedrich, 14
nostalgia, 93–94
numbing, 7
numinous, 34–40
   loss of, 99–100, 104
   see also divinity

Odysseus, 74, 106
old age, 114–29
   fear, 122–23
   personal authority, 127–28
   personal liberation and taking risks, 124–25
   questions to ask yourself, 126–27
   shut up, suit up, show up, 116
   see also mortality
Olympus, 94, 99–100
otherness. *See* shadow concept
overwhelment, 7–8

Pan, 97
parent complexes, 83, 86–89

passages, 20–21
   destiny, keeping our appointment with, 24–31
   in-between times, 97–98
   middle passages, 23–24
   reconstructing map of self and world, 31–34
   rites of passage, 20–21
   see also midlife crises
patterns, 2–3, 16
   presences, 78–79
   self-defeating, 9
   solving versus outgrowing, 120
personal authority, 58, 127–28
personality, 24–25
postmodernity, 104
power and power complexes, 7–9, 32, 86, 90–91
presences, 78–79
pride, 68–69
procrastination, 7
projection, 4, 6
   five stages of, 32–33
   magical other, 32
   shadow modality, 48–49
psyche, 3, 12, 16, 108, 146–47
   diverse and divided, 48
   timelessness of, 77
   see also ego
psychopathology, 12–13

repression, 7, 11, 65
resonance, 128
Rilke, Rainer Maria, 34–35, 39, 69–70, 107–8, 117–19, 129, 135

self, 4, 16–17, 107
   false self, 26, 44

sense of self, 4–5
   see also ego; psyche; unconscious
self-esteem, 8–9
self-estrangement, 11, 143
shadow concept, 41–60
   anxiety, 43–44, 66
   collective shadow, 45–47
   confronting, 50–52
   evil, 41–42
   modalities, 47–49
   positive shadow, 44
   questions to explore your shadow side, 55–59
   see also sins
Shakespeare, William, 70–71
shame, 91–92
shut up, suit up, show up, 116
Singularity, 103–4
sins, 61–62, 74–76
   anger, 66–68
   envy, 69–71
   gluttony, 62–64
   greed, 71–73
   lust, 64–66
   pride, 68–69
   sloth, 74
sloth, 74
Socratic fallacy, 75
soul, 80, 105–8, 146
   see also psyche
"The Soul and Death" (Jung), 138–41
spirits. *See* ghosts/hauntings
splinter selves and scripts, 2, 48
"stirring the process," 15–17
stories (of the self), 2, 5–6
suppression, 7

therapy, 10, 12, 31, 106
therapeuein, 12, 106
Thomas, Dylan, 131–32
thresholds, 24
Tolstoy, Leo, 139
tragedy, 24
transference, 6

unconscious, 1–2, 51, 78–79, 121, 141
    shadow self, 47–48
    see also dreams; projection

vocation, 13–14, 35

Wakoski, Diane, 77, 81, 85, 91, 96

Yeats, William Butler, 98, 124–26, 132, 140

Zagajewski, Adam, 81
Zeus, 99–100
Zorn, Fritz, 67

About the Author

James Hollis, PhD, was born in Springfield, Illinois, graduated from Manchester and Drew Universities and the Jung-Institut of Zurich, and lives in Washington, DC, with his wife, Jill. Together they have three living children and eight grandchildren. For the last half century, he has been devoted to sharing the insights of depth psychology via lectures on six continents, eighteen books, and countless courses, as well as conducting an analytic practice. Additionally, he has been instrumental in the formation and administration of Jung Institutes and Centers in Philadelphia, Houston, and Washington, DC.

About Sounds True

Sounds True is a multimedia publisher whose mission is to inspire and support personal transformation and spiritual awakening. Founded in 1985 and located in Boulder, Colorado, we work with many of the leading spiritual teachers, thinkers, healers, and visionary artists of our time. We strive with every title to preserve the essential "living wisdom" of the author or artist. It is our goal to create products that not only provide information to a reader or listener but also embody the quality of a wisdom transmission.

For those seeking genuine transformation, Sounds True is your trusted partner. At SoundsTrue.com you will find a wealth of free resources to support your journey, including exclusive weekly audio interviews, free downloads, interactive learning tools, and other special savings on all our titles.

To learn more, please visit SoundsTrue.com/freegifts or call us toll-free at 800.333.9185.

sounds true
WAKING UP THE WORLD